PRE-INTERMEDIATE

Language LEADER
WORKBOOK
and Audio CD

Ian Lebeau   Gareth Rees

CONTENTS

CONTENTS

Listening	Spelling / Pronunciation	Scenario	Study & Writing skills
A conversation about winter in Australia **DICTATION**	Spelling: Double letters Pronunciation: intonation	**Key language:** Agreeing/ disagreeing	Using your dictionary (understanding meaning) A guidebook entry **TRANSLATION**
Interview with Krzysztof Kiewlowski **LISTEN BETTER:** Activating your knowledge **DICTATION**	Spelling: Common mistakes Pronunciation: Word stress	**Key language:** Describing people	Learning styles Keeping a learning diary
Four monologues about the media **LISTEN BETTER:** Identifying the general topic **DICTATION**	Spelling: Plural forms Pronunciation: Sentence stress	**Key language:** Making suggestions	Working with others A TV programme review **TRANSLATION**
LISTEN BETTER: Hearing the present perfect **DICTATION**	Spelling: Past participles Pronunciation: Intonation in yes/no questions	**Key Language:** Giving advice and reasons	Guessing the meaning of unknown words A thank-you email **TRANSLATION**
Radio programme – holiday events **LISTEN BETTER:** Listening for specific information **DICTATION**	Spelling: Geographical names Pronunciation: Weak forms and schwa	**Key language:** Describing photographs	Time management A comparative essay **TRANSLATION**
Current affairs discussion **DICTATION**	Spelling: Vowels Pronunciation: *What'll* Pronunciation: Word linking (consonant to vowel)	**Key language:** Expressing opinions	Correcting your writing An article **TRANSLATION**
Careers advice **DICTATION**	Spelling: Difficult words Pronunciation: Voiced and unvoiced consonants	**Key language:** Developing an argument	Making notes Describing charts **TRANSLATION**
A talk on the Moon **LISTEN BETTER:** Signposts **DICTATION**	Spelling: Silent letters Pronunciation: Intonation in *Wh*- questions	**Key language:** Expressing preference	Improving your memory A story **TRANSLATION**
A talk on South African economy **LISTEN BETTER:** Staying cool **DICTATION**	Spelling: Plural forms Nouns ending -*er* or -*or* Pronunciation: /s/ or /z/	**Key language:** Negotiating	Giving a short talk Describing a process **TRANSLATION**
A student talk **LISTEN BETTER:** Taking notes **DICTATION**	Spelling: People and organisations Pronunciation: Pausing and emphatic stress	**Key language:** Adding emphasis	Improving your listening A for and against essay **TRANSLATION**
A talk on recycling systems in Auckland New Zealand **LISTEN BETTER:** Synonyms **DICTATION**	Spelling: Adjectives Pronunciation: Intonation in question tags	**Key language:** Question tags	Exploring reading texts A report **TRANSLATION**
Five monologues about sport **LISTEN BETTER:** Understanding emotion and feeling **DICTATION**	Spelling: Nouns Pronunciation: Intonation in lists	**Key language:** Conversation fillers	Doing exams A formal email **TRANSLATION**

Weather

1.1 EXTREMES

VOCABULARY: the weather

1 Are these words nouns (n) or adjectives (adj)?

1	dry	_adj_	8	rainy	_____
2	snow	_____	9	hot	_____
3	windy	_____	10	rain	_____
4	humid	_____	11	wet	_____
5	fog	_____	12	cloudy	_____
6	ice	_____	13	sun	_____
7	warm	_____	14	wind	_____

2 Choose the correct word to complete the sentences.

1 I always take my umbrella on ~~dry~~/rainy days.

2 The airport is closed because of the *fog/humid*.

3 I love watching the *snow/ice* fall from the sky.

4 Look! The *wind/windy* is blowing the leaves from the trees.

5 Put the air-conditioning on. It's very *sun/hot* in here.

6 It's a lovely *warm/cloudy* day. Let's go to the beach.

7 Listen to the sound of the *wet/rain* on the window. It's very loud.

GRAMMAR: present simple and present continuous

3 Choose the correct form of the verb to complete the sentences.

1 He always ~~go~~/goes to Jamaica in the winter for the sun.

2 Today I *am/is* working from home because of the heavy snow.

3 I *don't/doesn't* like humid days. They're so uncomfortable.

4 The snow *aren't/isn't* falling now. Let's go outside for a walk.

5 She *don't/doesn't* usually drive in the fog because it's dangerous.

6 We *are/is* still waiting for the rain to stop.

4 Complete this Internet blog about a hurricane with the correct form of the verbs in brackets.

Monday 10 a.m.

Hi, everyone. Today, I
¹*am writing* (write) from a city under attack from a hurricane! As you know, I
² _____ (live) in the city centre. The streets
³ _____ (be) usually busy at this time of day, but today they ⁴ _____ (be) empty.

Monday 11 a.m.

I ⁵ _____ still _____ (wait) for the hurricane to hit, but right now the winds ⁶ _____ (get) stronger and the rain ⁷ _____ (hit) the windows. It's so noisy!

Monday 11.30 a.m.

It's here! Amazing! Trees ⁸ _____ (fly) down the street. The noise ⁹ _____ (be) incredible. I
¹⁰ _____ (sit) on the floor behind my table in case the windows break.

Monday 2.30 p.m.

Incredible! Right now, the street ¹¹ _____ (turn) into a river. This ¹² _____ usually _____ (not happen). The water ¹³ _____ (carry) cars down the street!

Monday 3.30 p.m.

The water level ¹⁴ _____ still _____ (rise). I
¹⁵ _____ (not know) what to do. At the moment, the police ¹⁶ _____ (not answer) the phone.

Monday 4.30 p.m.

The water is very near to my second floor flat. This is my last message today – I ¹⁷ _____ (go) to the roof now! Wish me luck!

TRANSLATION

5 Translate into your language. Notice the differences.

1 I travel to work by train every day.

_____

2 He's reading an English book.

_____

3 It isn't raining now.

_____

4 She usually gives us homework on Fridays.

_____

5 They're waiting for the bus.

_____

READ BETTER: keep reading

When you read a text for the first time, don't worry about every difficult word. Finish the text before you check words in your dictionary.

- Don't keep stopping to use your dictionary; keep reading.

6 When you read the text in Exercise 7a for the first time, don't check new words in your dictionary. Wait until Exercise 7b.

READING

7a Read the text and put the headings in the correct spaces 1–5.

> ~~Weather forecasting – why we do it~~
> Collecting the information   Improving accuracy
> How nature can help   Using the information

7b Read the text again and choose six words that you want to check in a dictionary.

1 _____   4 _____

2 _____   5 _____

3 _____   6 _____

1 _Weather forecasting – why we do it_

Weather forecasts help ordinary people plan their daily life, but accurate forecasts are more important for farmers and sailors. Farmers can decide when to collect their crops and sailors can plan for storms.

2 _____

The natural world can help us forecast the weather. For example, this is a popular saying: 'Red sky at night, sailor's delight. Red sky in the morning, sailor's warning.' The red night sky means good weather the next day. The red morning sky means bad weather later that day.

3 _____

Most weather data comes from small weather stations on land which measure wind speed, air pressure, temperature and rainfall. Scientists also use weather balloons to collect the same information from high in the atmosphere.

4 _____

Nowadays, satellites provide useful measurements and images. This information helps us understand how weather works and this means we can make better forecasts with fewer mistakes.

5 _____

Scientists use the data from weather stations and satellites to make forecasts. They also use it to create different models of the atmosphere. However, they still can't predict the weather more than five days in advance.

8 Are these sentences about the text in Exercise 7 true or false?

1 Farmers don't need weather forecasts. _false_

2 Sailors prefer a red sky in the evening. _____

3 Weather balloons don't measure wind speed.

_____

4 Satellite pictures are useful for weather forecasters.

_____

5 Scientists make good forecasts for two-week periods. _____

VOCABULARY: words from the lesson

1 Tick the words and phrases that are about winter.

1 a documentary — ——
2 minus 10 degrees Celsius ✔
3 freezing winds ——
4 health benefits ——
5 heavy snow ——
6 a luxury ——
7 a community event ——
8 fur coats ——
9 sub-zero temperatures ——
10 icy water ——

VOCABULARY: modifiers

2 Look at the chart. Complete the sentences with the words in the box.

	°C	°F			°C	°F	
Algiers	18	64	f	Nairobi	22	72	f
Bangkok	32	90	f	New York	3	37	c
Beijing	0	32	s	Perth	37	99	s
Beirut	16	61	s	Rio de Jan	31	88	c
Cairo	18	64	c	Riyadh	19	66	s
Harare	27	81	s	San Fran	7	45	s
Hong Kong	19	66	f	Santiago	31	88	s
Istanbul	10	50	c	Sao Paulo	30	86	c
Jeddah	24	75	s	Seychelles	27	81	sh
Jerusalem	17	63	f	Singapore	24	75	r
Jo'burg	27	81	s	Sydney	28	82	s
Karaci	25	77	f	Taipi	19	66	dr
L Angeles	12	54	f	Tenerife	24	75	c
Manila	31	88	f	Toronto	7	45	c
Miami	23	73	c	Vancouver	-5	23	c
Mombasa	31	88	f	Washington	9	48	r
N Orleans	22	72	c	Wellington	16	61	f

Key: c=cloud, dr=drizzle, ds=dust storm, f=fair, fg=fog, g=gales, h=hail,
m=mist, r=rain, sh=showers, sl=sleet, sn=snow, s=sun, th=thunder, w=windy.
Forecast/readings for noon

~~very/really~~	extremely	quite

1 It's *very/really* cold in Beijing.
2 It's _____ cold in Istanbul.
3 It's _____ cold in Vancouver.

SPELLING: double letters

3 Choose the correct spelling.

1 ~~afect~~ / affect
2 diferent / different
3 familiar / familliar
4 gases / gasses
5 milions / millions
6 Rusia / Russia

LISTENING

4 **1.2** **Listen to the conversation about winter in Australia and answer the questions.**

1 What are the winter months in Australia?
   From May or June to August.

2 Where are winters chilly, with short days?
   _____

3 Does it snow a lot in the cities?
   _____

4 Where are the mountains with a lot of snow?
   _____

5 When is a very popular time for skiing in these mountains?
   _____

6 Why do some people go to New Zealand?
   _____

7 What percentage of Australia is tropical?
   _____

8 What can you do in the north of Australia in winter?
   _____

DICTATION

5 [1.3] **Listen and complete the text.**

A university lecturer in Wales believes that 24 January is a very bad day for a lot of people. _____

_____

_____

_____

_____

since Christmas and the fun of Christmas and New Year is just a distant memory. People are not keeping their New Year resolutions and _____

_____

_____

and have a sense of failure. The lecturer, Cliff Arnalls of Cardiff University, even has a formula for it.

GRAMMAR: present simple and present continuous questions

6 **Read the comments and write questions using the words.**

'I always go on holiday in January. This year, it's two weeks in the Caribbean! Bye!'
Shilpa
_____

'I love winter. I love the really cold winds and fresh snow.'
Julie
_____

'Hey! Excuse me – 24 January is my birthday. It's always a great day for me!'
Stella
_____

'For me, January is OK. It's August I hate – when I go back to work after my summer holiday.'
Chris
_____

'Move to Australia – it's summer there!'
Jay
_____

'When the weather's bad, I watch an old film – like a comedy or a musical. It's a good way to feel better.'
Alex

1 When / Shilpa / holiday?
  When does Shilpa (usually) go on holiday?

2 Why / Julie / love?
  _____

3 Why / Stella / 24 January?
  _____

4 Which month / Chris / hate?
  _____

5 Where / summer / January?
  _____

6 What kind / films / Alex / weather / bad?
  _____

7 **Answer these questions about winter in your country. Use short answers, Yes, I do / No, he doesn't, etc.**

1 Does winter start in November?
  Yes, it does. / No, it doesn't.

2 Does it often snow?
  _____

3 Are winters getting warmer?
  _____

4 Do you wear fur coats or hats?
  _____

5 Does the temperature ever drop to minus 60 degrees Celsius?
  _____

6 Do children sometimes have lessons on TV because they can't go to school?
  _____

8 **Correct the punctuation using capital letters, commas, apostrophes and full stops. There are three sentences.**

a lot of people dont like winter but I dont mind the freezing winds snow and ice im a big winter sports fan and I usually go skiing in france austria or switzerland with my friends sam and jo february is my favourite winter month

_____

_____

_____

_____

VOCABULARY: adventure holiday activities

1 Make compound nouns with the words in the box.

| cruise diving horse kayaking mountain |
| riding snow trekking white-water |

1 wildlife *cruise*

2 sea _____

3 _____ rafting

4 jungle _____

5 _____ biking

6 _____ boarding

7 _____ riding

8 scuba _____

2 Answer these questions about the vocabulary in Exercise 1.

1 Which activity needs very cold weather?

   snowboarding

2 Which activity do you do underwater?

   _____

3 Which activities do you do in the sea or on a river?

   _____, _____ and

   _____

4 Which activity needs a bicycle?

   _____

5 Which activity needs an animal?

   _____

6 Which activity needs a pair of walking boots?

   _____

KEY LANGUAGE: agreeing/disagreeing

3a Complete the conversation about adventure holidays with the words in the box.

| do   don't   neither   so |

CARLA: I think the trip to Southern Argentina sounds interesting.

ROSA: ¹ *So* do I. I'd really like to go there. But I'm not sure about the weather. I hate cold, windy weather.

CARLA: ² _____ you? I don't. I mean, it's okay if you have the right clothes. I don't want to go somewhere hot.

ROSA: ³ _____ you? I do. I'm interested in the trip to Belize.

CARLA: Well, I think the jungle is too hot for me. What about Chile?

ROSA: I don't like the activities on that holiday.

CARLA: ⁴ _____ do I. I hate mountain biking. I always fall off!

ROSA: ⁵ _____ do I! Perhaps Peru is the best choice. We can go white-water rafting. I really want to do that.

CARLA: Do you? I ⁶ _____. I think it's very dangerous. But I like horse riding. I can do that while you go rafting.

ROSA: Okay, so let's go to Peru. I really need a holiday.

CARLA: So ⁷ _____ I!

3b 🔲1.4 Listen and check your answers.

PRONUNCIATION: intonation

4 🔲1.5 Listen and repeat the phrases in Exercise 3. Match them to the intonation patterns in the table.

high start, fall	high start, fall, rise
1	

1 Look at the word. Then match the definitions 1–3 with the sentences a–c.

1 cool

  1 the opposite of warm

  2 fashionable and popular

  3 calm, not nervous

  a) It was hot in the day, but cool at night. _1_

  b) She tried to stay cool and not panic. _____

  c) Levi jeans are still cool today. _____

2 fine

  1 healthy and happy

  2 sunny and pleasant weather

  3 good quality

  a) we sell fine food from around the world. _____

  b) I hope the weather stays fine for the picnic. _____

  c) 'How's your mother?' 'She's fine, thanks.' _____

3 clear

  1 easy to understand

  2 you can see through something easily

  3 without clouds

  a) What a lovely day, the sky is completely clear.

  _____

  b) Some of the questions in the exam weren't clear.

  _____

  c) Does your car have clear or black tinted windows? _____

WRITING SKILLS: a guidebook entry

2 Complete the guidebook entry about Norway with the words in the box.

| also | and | but | when |

Norway
When to go

Norway has four wonderful seasons [1] _and_ there are places to visit all year round.

Spring

[2] _____ the weather gets warmer after the long winter you can experience the Norwegian Fjords by boat. At this time of the year, the waterfalls are strong [3] _____ dramatic because the winter snow is melting. The days are warmer, [4] _____ you need to bring an umbrella!

Summer

People think that Norway is a cold country all year round, [5] _____ in fact the temperatures can reach 25–30 degrees C during the summer. This is the ideal time to visit the sandy beaches of southern Norway. There are [6] _____ many beautiful lakes where you can swim [7] _____ go sailing.

Autumn

This is a quiet time in Norway [8] _____ it is one of the best times to visit because the countryside is very beautiful. The trees change to wonderful colours [9] _____ autumn comes. The air is [10] _____ clear and fresh. This means it is the perfect time to go mountain trekking.

Winter

[11] _____ the temperature drops, Norway becomes a special place to visit. In the mountain areas you can go skiing [12] _____ snowboarding. It is [13] _____ the ideal time to visit the north of Norway – the Arctic region. [14] _____ the weather is right [15] _____ the nights are long, you can see the spectacular Northern Lights – an unforgettable experience.

3a Read the text again. Find 18 adjectives and write them in your notebook.

3b Write sentences in your notebook to describe some places you know.

2 People

2.1 INSPIRATION

VOCABULARY: personality adjectives

1 Complete the adjectives in each sentence.

1 Picasso was a very t _a_ l _e_ _n_ t _e_ d artist.

2 My manager is __ a __ d-w __ __ k __ __ __. He often works late.

3 I don't like her. She's not very f r __ __ n __ __ y.

4 He's h __ l __ __ __ l. Ask him for advice.

5 She never stops trying. She is very d __ __ e __ __ i __ __ d.

6 You are very k __ __ __. Thank you for your help.

7 Teachers need to be very p __ t i __ n __.

8 My boss is a good leader. He's i __ s p __ r __ __ i o __ __ __.

9 She's l __ v __ __ __. I'd like to see her again.

10 She is a d __ __ i __ __ t __ d nurse.

GRAMMAR: past simple

2 Complete the stories about famous inspirational people. Use the verbs in the boxes.

arrest	change	~~get~~	not get	tell

Rosa Parks

On 1 December 1955, in Alabama USA, Rosa Parks a young African American woman, ¹ _got_ on a bus and made history. The bus driver ² _____ her to get out of her seat because a white man needed it. She ³ _____ out of her seat and the police ⁴ _____ her. This started a massive protest and, after one year, the local government ⁵ _____ the law. Finally, black and white people were able to travel together.

become	not be	not make	sail	take

Michael Perham

In January 2007, Michael Perham, a young British boy aged 14, ⁶ _____ across the Atlantic Ocean and into the history books. He ⁷ _____ the youngest person to sail across this ocean – on his own. There ⁸ _____ anyone else with him on the boat and he ⁹ _____ any stops during the journey. This incredible journey across the Atlantic Ocean ¹⁰ _____ seven weeks.

become	lead	not become	organise
spend			

Mahatma Ghandi

In the early 1900s, Mahatma Ghandi was an Indian lawyer who ¹¹ _____ peaceful protests against the British rulers. In 1930, he ¹² _____ thousands of people on a 400km march to protest against heavy taxes. During his life he ¹³ _____ seven years in prison, but finally in 1947, India ¹⁴ _____ independent. He ¹⁵ _____ the president of India, but he was called the Father of the Nation.

3 Complete the questions with the verbs in box A. You may need to add a question word from box B.

A	be	go	sell	spend	~~travel~~

B	~~how~~	when	where	why

1 _How_ _did_ you _travel_ to college yesterday?
  By bus.

2 _____ _____ you last _____ on holiday?
  In June. I went to Florida in the USA.

3 _____ Sarah _____ much money yesterday?
  Yes, she did. She bought lots of clothes.

4 _____ _____ you last night?

I was at my friend's house. She cooked dinner for me.

5 _____ _____ he _____ his car last week?

Because he needed some money!

READING

4 Read the article from *Management Monthly*. How many key characteristics of modern managers are there? What are they?

_____

_____

_____

_____

What makes a modern manager?

The modern manager works in a very different way compared to the manager of the past. Are you a modern manager or are you stuck in the past?

5 First of all, a modern manager should be inspirational. In the past, managers gave out tasks and expected people to do them, without asking questions. Nowadays, you need to encourage your staff members. Tell them why their tasks are important for
10 the company and thank them for good work.

Secondly, you should be well-organised. Previously, the secretary managed the daily schedules and weekly plans. The secretary wrote the letters and posted them. Now, we have email, so you can't give all this
15 work to your secretary. At the end of every day, check the plan for the next day. Make sure <u>you</u> know it well. You should also be hard-working. Perhaps, in the past, senior managers had extra-long lunch breaks, or they finished early on Fridays. Modern
20 managers set good examples for their staff and concentrate on their work. Make sure you don't leave the office first.

Finally, you should be friendly. Previously, managers stayed behind their desks or only went for lunch
25 with other managers. Nowadays, managers are more friendly. Leave your office and walk around the company. Talk to your staff and have lunch with them during the week.

5 Complete the sentences using the verb phrases in the box.

| know the weekly schedule |
| not explain why a task is important |
| not go home early   rely on the secretary |
| stay in his/her office   use email |

1 A manager in the past didn't explain why a task is important.

A manager in the past _____.

A manager in the past _____.

2 A modern manager _____.

A modern manager _____.

A modern manager _____.

6 Find these words in the text. What do they refer to?

1 them (line 7)   <u>tasks</u>

2 them (line 9)   _____

3 them (line 10)   _____

4 them (line 14)   _____

5 it (line 17)   _____

6 them (line 27)   _____

SPELLING

7 Each word has one missing letter. Correct the words.

1 profesional   <u>professional</u>

2 athlets   _____

3 suceed   _____

4 brekfast   _____

5 lovly   _____

6 prepar   _____

7 nervos   _____

8 equpment   _____

9 kilometrs   _____

10 vilage   _____

VOCABULARY:
words from the lesson

1 Match the words with the pictures 1–7.

| acting | dancing | drawing | painting |
| playing music | singing | writing stories | |

1 _playing music_

2 _____

3 _____

4 _____

5 _____

6 _____

7 _____

EXTRA VOCABULARY:
nationality adjectives

2a Complete the table with nationality adjectives.

Country	Nationality adjective
Australia	_Australian_
Brazil	_Brazilian_
China	_____
Egypt	_____
France	_French_
Italy	_____
Japan	_____
Mexico	_____
Poland	_____

Country	Nationality adjective
Russia	_____
Spain	_____
Switzerland	_____
Turkey	_____
the Netherlands (Holland)	_____
the UK	_____
the USA	_____

2b Write the correct nationality for each person. Use the words in Exercise 2a.

1 Pablo Picasso. A _Spanish_ painter.

2 Akira Kurosawa. A _____ film director.

3 Naguib Mahfouz. An _____ writer.

4 Frank Lloyd Wright. An _____ architect.

5 Gianni Versace. An _____ fashion designer.

EXTRA VOCABULARY:
adjectives ending in *-ful*

3 Complete the sentences with the words in the box.

| beautiful | careful | cheerful | colourful |
| painful | peaceful | powerful | successful |

1 Be _careful_ when you cross the road. It's very busy.

2 He's a very _____ man – always smiling.

3 There's no traffic in her street. It's very

_____.

4 The view from the top of the building was

_____.

5 They're a _____ couple. He's a rich lawyer and she's a famous architect.

6 I hurt my arm playing tennis. Now it's quite

_____.

7 The tram is red, yellow and green. It's really

_____.

8 The President of the USA is a very

_____ person.

When you listen, use your knowledge of the world and your own experience of life to help you understand and guess the right answers.

4 Use your knowledge of the world to choose the correct answers a), b) or c).

1 When was John Harrison, the inventor of the first accurate clock, born?

   a) 1693   b) 1893   c) 1963

2 When did the last man walk on the moon?

   a) 1090   b) 1969   c) 1972

LISTENING

5a `1.6` Look at these events in the life of the Polish film director Krzysztof Kiewlowski. Listen and put them in order 1–6.

1 He made his first short films. ____

2 He went to film school. ____

3 He was born in Warsaw in 1941.   _1_

4 He made documentaries about ordinary people. ____

5 He made some films outside Poland. ____

6 His family lived in different places. ____

5b `1.6 and 1.7` Listen to the interview again. Choose a statement a–c to describe the films 1–4.

Films

1 *A Short Film about Love* ____

2 *A Short Film about Killing* ____

3 *The Double Life of Veronique* ____

4 *Three Colours: Blue, White and Red* ____

Statements

a) '… about two women, one in Poland, one in France.'

b) '… about being free, being equal and being kind to people.'

c) '… about the lives of people in one building.'

DICTATION

6 `1.8` Listen and write the text in your notebook.

GRAMMAR: past continuous and past simple

7a Choose the correct form of the verbs.

Simone de Beauvoir (1908–1986) was a French writer and philosopher. She was born in Paris. In 1929, when she ¹*studied / was studying* at the University of the Sorbonne, she ²*met / was meeting* Jean-Paul Sartre. De Beauvoir and Sartre ³*started / were starting* a relationship that ⁴*was lasting / lasted* for life. Sartre later ⁵*became / was becoming* the major French philosopher of the twentieth century. In the 1930s and early 1940s, de Beauvoir was teaching in high schools in different French cities and at the Sorbonne. All this time, she ⁶*was developing / wasn't developing* her ideas about philosophy and about the position of women in society. In 1949 her book *The Second Sex* ⁷*was appearing / appeared*. It ⁸*was becoming / became* a very important book for women in the 1970s. De Beauvoir travelled a lot, often with Sartre, and visited Portugal, Italy, China and the USA. Jean-Paul Sartre ⁹*died / was dying* in 1980. In 1981 de Beauvoir ¹⁰*was writing / wrote* a painful book about his last years.

7b Complete these questions about Simone de Beauvoir, using the past continuous. Then write answers.

1 Where *was she studying* in 1929?

   At the University of the Sorbonne, in Paris.

2 Where _____ (live) in the 1930s and early 1940s?

   _____

3 In the early 1930s and 1940s, where _____ (teach)?

   _____

4 What _____ (develop) in the 1930s and early 1940s?

   _____

VOCABULARY: describing people

1 Write the letters in the correct order to make the opposite of the adjectives.

1 cheerful	lembrasie	m _iserable_
2 friendly	drneiylfnu	u_____
3 quiet	tyhcta	c_____
4 clever	pitsud	s_____
5 shy	tiencofdn	c_____
6 smart	cyfrfsu	s_____
7 rude	lptioe	p_____
8 lazy	darh-knwroig	h_____
9 nice	lehorbri	h_____

2 Complete the sentences with phrases in the box.

> a good cook   do the washing up
> good-looking   honest   rich
> similar interests   smoke

1 Come round for dinner. My flatmate's _a good cook._

2 She cooks and then I _____.

3 We have _____. For example, we both like sports.

4 There aren't any cigarettes in the house. We don't _____.

5 We have a small flat because we aren't _____.

6 I trust her because she seems _____.

7 He isn't ugly, he's very _____.

PRONUNCIATION: word stress

3a Match the adjectives from Exercise 1 to these stress patterns.

1 Oo	2 oO	3 oOo	4 Ooo	5 Oooo
friendly				

3b `1.9` Listen and check your answers.

KEY LANGUAGE: describing people

4a Read the answers and complete the questions.

1 _What does he look like?_
He's got short blond hair and he's tall.

2 _____ she _____?
She's really nice – very friendly and chatty.

3 _____ food _____ they _____?
Oh, they eat anything … with chips!

4 _____ you _____ a coffee?
Yes, please. One sugar thank you.

5 _____ _____ you _____ doing in your free time?
I love going to the cinema, and playing badminton.

6 _____ she _____ _____ anyone famous?
Well, I think she looks like Nicole Kidman.

7 _____ _____ you _____ to do tonight?
I think I'd like to go to the theatre. What's on?

8 _____ _____ your kids _____
_____?
They've both got brown hair, and they're scruffy!

9 _____ your new boss _____?
She's very hard-working.

10 _____ your father _____ you?
Yes, he is. We're both very sociable.

4b `1.10` Listen and check your answers.

PUNCTUATION

5 Correct the punctuation using capital letters, commas, apostrophes and full stops. There are four sentences.

coco chanel was a famous french fashion designer she opened her first shop in 1912 in 1922 she introduced a perfume called chanel no 5 she was still working when she died in 1971

_____

_____

_____

_____

<table>
<tr><td>

STUDY SKILLS: learning styles and strategies

1 **Look at the statements and answer the questions.**

1 Which learning style do these statements refer to?

Auditory (hearing things)   A

Physical (doing things)   P

Visual (seeing things)   V

2 Are the statements positive or negative with regard to that learning style?

3 Are any of the statements true for you?

1 I always forget people's faces. It's very embarrassing!

V negative   No. I'm good at remembering people's faces.

2 I like it when course books use pictures to explain things.

_____

3 I always have my best ideas when I'm doing some exercise.

_____

4 I can't stand lectures.

_____

5 I don't even know which way round to hold a map.

_____

6 I got some great audio books for my birthday.

_____

7 I learn new words by saying them aloud. It really works for me.

_____

8 I always read the instruction book before I use a new electronic device.

_____

9 I chose a science degree so that I could do experiments.

_____

10 Everyone says I can't keep my hands still when I'm talking.

_____

</td><td>

WRITING SKILLS: keeping a learning diary

2 **Read the text about exam preparation. Choose the correct words.**

We are now halfway through our IELTS exam preparation course and, ¹*at the moment / ~~at first~~*, I am feeling more confident about the exam. ²*Afterwards / At first*, I was really worried because there was a lot to learn about the exam. For example, in the reading paper there are lots of different question types. I was really confused by all this ³*until / at first* our teacher gave us some tips on how to answer them.

We did a practice interview yesterday. ⁴*Until / Afterwards* my teacher told me that my accent is a bit strong, but I speak accurately. ⁵*At the moment / Afterwards*, I'm probably most worried about the listening paper because you only hear each listening text once, ⁶*then / at first* you have a very short time to answer some difficult questions.

⁷*Until / At first*, I found the writing quite difficult, but ⁸*then / at first* our teacher showed us how to plan our writing for the opinion essay. First of all, you should read the question carefully and underline the key words. ⁹*At first / Then* you should write down some ideas ¹⁰*until / afterwards* you have four or five good points. ¹¹*Until / Afterwards,* you should organise the ideas, perhaps into positives and negatives, and ¹²*then / until* plan each paragraph. Finally, you write the essay. Good advice!

3 **In your notebook describe three things you did and learnt in your recent English classes.**

</td></tr>
</table>

3 The media

3.1 MY MEDIA

VOCABULARY: the media

1 Match the phrases 1–8 with a–h to make sentences and questions.

1 Did you play

2 It's a good advert but

3 Latin American soap operas

4 She left her job because

5 Do journalists

6 He writes articles

7 *Big Brother* is

8 There was an interesting documentary

a) on Channel 7 last night. ____

b) she received 300 emails a day. ____

c) usually tell the truth? ____

d) for his university newspaper. ____

e) are very popular in Spain. ____

f) I can't remember the name of the product. ____

g) a lot of computer games when you were 15? _1_

h) a reality TV show. ____

SPELLING: plural forms

2 Write the plural forms of these words.

1 woman   *women*

2 series   _____

3 celebrity   _____

4 search engine   _____

5 dress   _____

6 radio   _____

7 copy   _____

READING

3 Read this webpage. Find one sentence that does not fit with the rest of the text.

About me

Hello! Welcome to my website. My name is Yuki and I'm Japanese. I'm a student of Art & Design in London. I'm really enjoying this city – it's expensive but it's never boring. I go everywhere by bike. In my free time, I like playing squash. I also like watching comedies on TV and writing material for my website – so I can practise my English! Please read my articles about some cultural events in London at the moment.

Hogarth
Tate Britain, London SW1, until 29 April

William Hogarth was a very successful English painter of the eighteenth century. He spent his life in London. All his famous paintings are in this enormous exhibition and there's a lot of variety. The paintings are full of life and some are very funny, but sometimes the amount of detail is confusing. Actually, I liked his prints more than the paintings. I was surprised by the way her beauty changes – sometimes she looks like Marilyn Monroe, sometimes like Katherine Hepburn. Anyway, this exhibition is definitely worth seeing. I now feel I understand a lot more about this city!

Kylie: The Exhibition
V&A, London SW7, until 10 June

Some people thought that a museum wasn't the right place for an exhibition about a modern celebrity's clothes. But some of the clothes we see are 20 years old, and *are* part of history. There's the white cotton dress Kylie wore for the video of *I Should Be So Lucky*. Then, there are the clothes she wore when she first appeared in the Australian soap opera *Neighbours*. Each dress, shoe or boot tells a story, and we learn about the designers, the videos, and the tours. The exhibition doesn't explain how she became so special but it's a lot of fun. I really recommend it!

4 Write the name of the exhibition (or exhibitions) which:

1 … is very big.   *Hogarth*

2 … is on in May.   _____

3 … helped Yuki learn about where she's living.   _____

4 … is about a successful person.   _____

5 … is really good and you should go and see it.   _____

5 Find words in the text that mean:

1 funny films or TV programmes (para 1)   *comedies*

2 when you aren't working (para 1)   _____

3 not interesting (para 1)   _____

4 when things are different from each other (para 2)   _____

5 a television programme about the lives of a group of people (para 3)   _____

6 a famous person, especially an actor or singer (para 3)   _____

GRAMMAR: articles

6 Read this text from an information leaflet for parents. Put *a*, *an*, *the* or no article in the gaps.

Keep your child safe on the Internet

Children love **¹** *the* **Internet**

It's ²_____ great way to have different kinds of fun, keep in touch with old friends and make new friends. They can also find ³_____ material for homework and sometimes buy ⁴_____ things like ⁵_____ music, ⁶_____ books or ⁷_____ games.

What are the risks?

Internet content

Most material on the Internet is legal, but it is easy for ⁸_____ children to see ⁹_____ images that are harmful to them. ¹⁰_____ children need to feel that they can talk to ¹¹_____ adult when they see something they don't like.

Internet contacts

Sometimes ¹²_____ children want to meet their Internet friends. Because you can't see ¹³_____ people you contact online, you have no idea who they are. It is not ¹⁴_____ good idea for ¹⁵_____ children to meet people from the Internet without ¹⁶_____ responsible adult. Explain to the child that ¹⁷_____ adult is not there to spoil their fun – it is just ¹⁸_____ basic safety.

DICTATION

7 [1.11] Listen and write the sentences.

1 _____

   _____

   _____

2 _____

   _____

   _____

3 _____

   _____

   _____

4 _____

   _____

   _____

VOCABULARY: nouns

1 Choose the correct noun to complete the sentences.

1 Cartier-Bresson was a famous French *photography/ photographer*.

2 I'm studying *science/scientist* at university.

3 Teachers should know a little about *psychology/ psychologist*.

4 Was Monet an *artist/art* or an author?

5 I think some *politicians/politics* want to improve the world.

6 A *journalist/journalism* wants to interview her about her company.

LISTEN BETTER: identifying the general topic

When you listen to something for the first time, try to identify the general topic or subject. You can try to understand the details when you listen to something for the second time.

• Use key words and phrases to identify the general topic.

2 Read the short extract and choose the best description 1–4. Which key words and phrases helped you?

'I went to university when I was 30 in order to study journalism. I was the oldest student on the course and at first it was difficult to get to know people. Then, I joined the Art Society and I met lots of lovely people.'

1 Improving study skills   _____

2 Working for a newspaper   _____

3 Making friends at work   _____

4 Making friends at college   _____

LISTENING

3 1.12 Listen to four people talking about the media. Which question is each person answering? There is one question that you do not need.

1 Speaker 1 answered question *b*

2 Speaker 2 answered question ____

3 Speaker 3 answered question ____

4 Speaker 4 answered question ____

a) What's your opinion of TV news programmes?

b) Do you think children should watch the news?

c) Are 24-hour news channels a good idea?

d) Do you get your news from the newspapers or from TV?

e) Which is better for news – newspapers or the Internet?

4 1.12 Listen again and choose the best ending a) or b) for each sentence.

1 Speaker 1 thinks that news about serious crimes:
  a) is okay for children to hear about.
  b) isn't okay for children to hear about.

2 Speaker 2 thinks that he can get more information from:
  a) newspapers than TV news programmes.
  b) TV news programmes than newspapers.

3 Speaker 3 is pleased that there are stories about:
  a) famous people from the entertainment world.
  b) stories from around the world.

4 Speaker 4 prefers:
  a) to get the news immediately things happen.
  b) to have stories with a lot of information and analysis.

GRAMMAR: relative pronouns

5 Read the sentence pairs and write *one* sentence using *who/that* or *that/which*.

1 a) The Times is a British newspaper.
   b) The Times is famous for its high standard of journalism.

   The Times is a British newspaper that/which is famous for its high standard of journalism.

2 a) Ryszard Kapuscinski was a Polish journalist.
   b) Ryszard Kapuscinski wrote books about Africa and the Middle East.

   _____

   _____

3 a) Rupert Murdoch is an Australian businessman.
   b) Rupert Murdoch owns media companies all over the world.

   _____

   _____

4 a) NewsAcademic.com is an international newspaper for young people.
   b) NewsAcademic.com is only available over the Internet.

   _____

   _____

5 a) Joseph Pulitzer was a Hungarian journalist.
   b) Joseph Pulitzer became editor of the biggest newspaper in the USA.

   _____

   _____

6 a) The Pulitzer Prizes are famous awards.
   b) The Pulitzer Prizes are for editors, journalists, photographers and cartoonists.

   _____

   _____

6 Complete these definitions. Use a word or phrase from the box with *who/that* or *that/which*.

| a company   a computer   a journalist |
| a person   a TV programme   a type of writing |

1 A film critic is *a person* *who/that* reviews movies.

2 A blog is _____ _____ is similar to a diary.

3 A chat show is _____ _____ shows interviews with famous people.

4 An editor is _____ _____ decides the content of a newspaper.

5 A laptop is _____ _____ you can easily carry.

6 A broadcaster is _____ _____ shows TV programmes.

VOCABULARY: words from the lesson

7 Read the definitions and complete the words.

1 An adjective or noun which means something is a different choice.

   a *l t e r n a t i v e*

2 The people who watch a TV programme.

   a _ _ _ _ _ _ _

3 An adjective that means someone has training and qualifications.

   p _ _ _ _ _ _ _ _ _ _

4 An adjective which means new and different.

   f _ _ _ _

5 An adjective which means many people like something.

   p _ _ _ _ _ _

6 An adjective which is similar to global.

   i _ _ _ _ _ _ _ _ _ _ _ _

7 A verb which means choose.

   s _ _ _ _ _

TRANSLATION

8 Translate into your language. Notice the differences.

1 John Logie Baird was the scientist that invented television.

   _____

2 CNN is an American TV channel which broadcasts all over the world.

   _____

3 Woodward and Bernstein were American journalists who discovered government secrets.

   _____

4 Youtube.com is a website that shows videos by ordinary people.

   _____

PRONUNCIATION: sentence stress

1 `1.13` **Listen to these TV extracts and underline the stressed words in each sentence.**

1 And <u>now</u>, <u>live</u> in the <u>studio</u>, it's <u>Danny</u> <u>Berlin</u> with his <u>latest</u> <u>song</u>, <u>Tears</u> Like <u>Autumn</u> <u>Leaves</u>.

2 Next, we have an interview with the Prime Minister and the results of our survey.

3 In the financial markets, the pound rose by ten pence against the dollar.

4 The lioness waits. She watches the deer and slowly moves through the grass.

5 This is what everyone is wearing this summer – the sleeveless T-shirt.

6 I love the work of Norman Foster. His buildings are modern and different.

7 The director is Stephen Spielberg, and the movie is typical of his work.

8 With powerful engines and no luggage space, the Ferrari has never been a family car.

9 TV presenter Sally Sweet went out last night with a new mystery man.

VOCABULARY: TV programme topics

2 **Match the TV extracts in Exercise 1 with the topics a–i.**

a) politics   _2_

b) pop music   ___

c) films   ___

d) business   ___

e) cars   ___

f) fashion   ___

g) celebrities and fame   ___

h) design   ___

i) nature and the environment   ___

KEY LANGUAGE: making suggestions

3a **Complete the conversation with words and phrases from the box.**

| any | ~~let's~~ | let's not | shall | should (x2) |
| what about (x2) | why don't |

MERYL: Right then everyone, [1] _let's_ hear your ideas for the next issue please. Tom?

TOM: Well, as it's the Oscars next week, [2] _____ we do an article about the fashion designers who work for the stars?

MERYL: Okay, I like that idea. Anyone else?

PAM: [3] _____ doing a piece that's more interesting for men?

MERYL: Sure. Such as?

PAM: Well, [4] _____ finding out what men think about female politicians? We could do a survey.

MERYL: Sounds good. I think we [5] _____ do something about food and diet. It's a hot topic at the moment. What about writing about people's lunch at work?

PAM: Interesting, but [6] _____ only look at office workers. We [7] _____ interview people with unusual jobs as well.

MERYL: Fine. Sasha, you're very quiet today. [8] _____ ideas?

SASHA: Not really. [9] _____ we finish the meeting now?

3b `1.14` **Listen and check your answers.**

STUDY SKILLS: working with others

1 Choose the correct word in each sentence.

1 Working with others ~~decreases~~/*increases* the amount of time each student talks in a lesson.

2 It helps students become *more/less* confident with the language.

3 It helps make students *more/less* independent as learners.

4 It *provides/reduces* variety in the lesson, which is good for learning.

5 Students learn interesting things from *the teacher/ other students*.

6 The teacher can *see/forget* how students are communicating and using the language.

2 Match the example phrases 1–11 with the language functions a–f.

1 Exactly. _a_

2 I think I agree with you, basically. ____

3 That's an interesting point. ____

4 Anyway, what do you think? ____

5 What do you mean, exactly? ____

6 I'm not sure I agree. ____

7 Are you saying that we should do it? ____

8 You're right. ____

9 Absolutely. ____

10 What do you think about 24-hour news? ____

11 Yes, but I don't think it's right. ____

a) Agreeing with your partner (x4)

b) Disagreeing with your partner (x2)

c) Asking for your partner's opinion (x2)

d) Checking your understanding

e) Asking for further explanation

f) Showing interest

WRITING SKILLS: a TV programme review

3 Read the TV programme review. Is the review positive or negative?

Party Animals
BBC 2

[1] *Politics and politicians dominate the news. Now, it's the turn of drama.* Party Animals is a comedy drama about the glamorous lives of some young researchers who work for the politicians in parliament. There are four main characters – three of them work for different political parties and one is a young political journalist. [2]_____.

They plan, they lie and they learn to use power to get what they want. They spend their free time in restaurants and at parties. [3]_____. These relationships are difficult because of the political differences.

Party Animals is a clever and entertaining comedy drama. [4]_____.

They are brilliant as ambitious, young and rather selfish people. [5]_____.

The script is convincing as well as funny. [6]_____.

4 Put these sentences a–f in the correct places 1–6 in the review.

a) Overall, this is a drama series to watch, even if you normally hate politics!

b) ~~Politics and politicians dominate the news. Now, it's the turn of drama.~~

c) The writer clearly knows about life behind the scenes of parliament.

d) At these parties, relationships develop between these ambitious characters.

e) These young graduates spend their working days in the Houses of Parliament.

f) The four main actors are all excellent.

Health

4.1 DOCTORS WITHOUT BORDERS

VOCABULARY: medical words (1)

1 Complete the sentences with the words in the box.

> clinic   disease   ~~illnesses~~   injuries
> malnutrition   medicine   nurses   operation
> surgeon   treatment

1 Most _illnesses_ in this area are minor now, so we are closing one of the clinics.

2 We urgently need money to buy _____, things like painkillers and antibiotics.

3 The bomb explosion has left people with terrible _____.

4 We have stopped the spread of _____ by cleaning everything well.

5 We have opened a new _____ in the jungle region.

6 A new _____ has arrived, so now we can do some of the operations.

7 Because of the lack of food, children are suffering from _____.

8 What's the best _____ for this illness – modern or traditional medicine?

9 He has a heart problem; he needs an _____.

10 Each night there are two doctors and four _____ on duty.

GRAMMAR: present perfect (1)

2 Correct the mistakes in these sentences. Use the present perfect.

1 I has worked in Chile and Peru.

  I have worked in Chile and Peru.

2 She have met you before.

  _____

3 They have ran health centres all over the world.

  _____

4 We didn't have finished the training course.

  _____

5 Did you have been to Tibet?

  _____

3 Complete these sentences using the past simple or the present perfect of the verbs in brackets.

1 So far today, I _have had_ (have) three cups of coffee.

2 This week we _____ (sell) five cars.

3 Last year there _____ (be) a hurricane in my country.

4 She _____ never _____ (thank) me for the help I gave.

5 In the last few days, you _____ (not do) any homework.

6 Six months ago, I _____ (travel) to the UK.

7 To date, there _____ (be) no accidents on this road.

8 Last year, I _____ (not go) on holiday.

9 _____ you ever _____ (see) a panda bear?

10 When _____ you last _____ (visit) your parents?

TRANSLATION

4 Translate into your language. Notice the differences.

1 I have seen many American films.

  _____

2 I went to the cinema last Saturday.

  _____

3 She has bought a new computer.

  _____

4 I have drunk four cups of coffee today.

  _____

5 He drank five cups of tea yesterday.

  _____

READ BETTER: topic sentences

Improve your understanding of a text by concentrating on the first sentence of each paragraph. This is usually the topic sentence. It tells you the main topic of the paragraph.

- When you read the rest of the paragraph, remember the topic. This will help you understand the new information or difficult words.

5 Look at the article about health care in Saudi Arabia. Read *only* the topic sentences of each paragraph. Then match paragraphs A–E with the topics 1–5. There is one topic that you do not need.

1 Difficulties for the health care system. ____

2 Why the nation's health is important. *A*

3 The philosophy of the Saudi system. ____

4 The organisation of the Saudi system. ____

5 The history of the health care system. ____

Health care in Saudi Arabia

A <u>The health of a country's population is an important responsibility of a government.</u> Illness, early deaths and serious disease weaken a country in both economic and social ways. As well as this, a nation needs to care for those people who can't care for themselves – the young and the elderly.

B <u>In the Kingdom of Saudi Arabia, the national health care system has two main sections which provide health care for the population.</u> Firstly, there is a nationwide network of health clinics. These clinics provide basic health services and emergency care. There are also some mobile clinics that regularly visit remote villages. Secondly, there is a network of 350 advanced hospitals and specialist clinics that are in urban areas across the country.

C <u>There are three basic principles or ideas that define the kingdom's health service.</u> First of all, everyone can receive care, including visitors to the country. Secondly, this care is free for everyone. When people are ill, they do not pay for their treatment. Finally, the money for the health service comes from the sale of the kingdom's oil.

D <u>The health care system continues to grow and develop, but it faces one particular problem.</u> A growing health system needs more and more doctors and nurses. Unfortunately, there are few medical colleges in Saudi Arabia, which means there are not many new Saudi doctors and nurses.

READING

6 Read the article again. Are these statements true, false, or does the text not say?

1 Poor mental health is a national problem. *doesn't say*

2 Small villages have some health care. _____

3 There are hospitals in the countryside. _____

4 Before 1932, only rich people could get health care. _____

5 The Saudi health service is better than in many other countries. _____

6 Only Saudi people can use the national health service. _____

7 When people are ill they get free treatment. _____

8 Saudi people do not want to become doctors. _____

9 Most employees of the health service are foreigners. _____

10 There will be more medical colleges for Saudi people. _____

7 Read the definitions and find words in the text with the same meanings.

1 the people in a country (para. A) *population*

2 to make something less strong (para. A) _____

3 not young (para. A) _____

4 all over the country (para. B) _____

5 the most (para. D) _____

The majority of the health workers in Saudi Arabia come from other countries. In order to solve this problem, the government is now building new medical training facilities.

VOCABULARY: medical words (2)

1 Complete the paragraph with the words in the box.

concentration	diet	disease	insomnia
mental	~~nutrition~~	physical	pressure
serious	vitamins		

Good [1] _nutrition_ and eating healthy food is essential for good health. Some food contains protein, e.g. meat, some food contains carbohydrates, e.g. pasta, and some food contains [2]_____, e.g. fruit. Our bodies need these things. However, other food contains a lot of sugar, e.g. chocolate, or a lot of fat, e.g. crisps. These foods can cause [3]_____ health problems such as high blood [4]_____ or heart disease. Food also influences our [5]_____ health, for example chocolate can change your mood. Vegetables and fish help reduce minor problems such as lack of [6]_____, poor memory and poor motivation. If you can't sleep ([7]_____), eat nuts. If you feel depressed, try eating brown rice. With regard to more [8]_____ illnesses, the Mediterranean [9]_____ may protect you from Alzheimer's [10]_____.

GRAMMAR: present perfect (2): for and since

2 Complete these time phrases with *for* or *since*.

1 _for_ three years
2 _____ yesterday
3 _____ an hour
4 _____ a week
5 _____ 2006
6 _____ I was 15 years old
7 _____ ages
8 _____ last January
9 _____ all my life

3 Complete these questions and answers. Use the present perfect form of *be*, *have* and *know* with *for* or *since*.

1 How long _have_ you _had_ your computer?
   I'_ve had_ it _for_ about a year.

2 How long _____ you _____ a student at this university?
   I _____ a student here _____ three years.

3 _____ you always _____ a lawyer?
   No, I _____ only _____ a lawyer _____ two years.

4 _____ you _____ each other for long?
   Yes, we _____. We _____ each other _____ we were children.

5 _____ she _____ green hair for long?
   No, she _____. She _____ it _____ a month or so.

6 _____ he always _____ a bad memory?
   Yes, he _____. He _____ a bad memory _____ years!

7 How long _____ he _____ in this country?
   He _____ here _____ 2005. That's when he left Mexico.

8 _____ you _____ how to drive for long?
   Yes, I _____. I passed my test eight years ago.

LISTEN BETTER: hearing the present perfect

Because we often use contractions when we use the present perfect: *I've*, *You've*, *He's*, *We've*, *They've*, it can be hard to hear this verb form. Sometimes, the difference between a present perfect and a past simple sentence is only very small, e.g. *to walk*, *walked*, *walked* or *to put*, *put*, *put*.

• Listen carefully for the contractions.
• Try to use the context to help you identify the present perfect.

4 Correct the punctuation in your notebook using capital letters, commas, apostrophes and full stops. There are three sentences.

before 1921 there wasnt a health service in saudi arabia in the 1930s king abdulaziz created a national health care system and by the 1970s there were 48000 hospital beds today it is in the top 30 of the world

5a [1.15] Listen and choose which sentence a) or b) you hear first.

1 a) I've had a lot to eat. ✓
   b) I had a lot to eat.

2 a) He's wanted to be a doctor for many years.
   b) He wanted to be a doctor for many years.

3 a) You've started a new book.
   b) You started a new book.

4 a) We've played tennis and football.
   b) We played tennis and football.

5 a) They've washed the car.
   b) They washed the car.

6 a) She's turned on the TV.
   b) She turned on the TV.

7 a) We've visited Denmark several times.
   b) We visited Denmark several times.

8 a) I've finished the exercise.
   b) I finished the exercise.

5b [1.15] Listen again and check your answers.

LISTENING

6 [1.16] Listen to a student talk to her careers adviser and answer these questions.

1 Which of these jobs do they discuss?
   a) a food scientist   b) a dietician   c) a doctor
   d) a nutritionist

2 Which job(s) does she decide to study?

_____

7 [1.16] Listen again. Are these statements true, false, or does the text not say?

1 Food scientists usually work in universities and hospitals. _false_

2 Food scientists are more important than nutritionists. _____

3 Food scientists change the appearance of food. _____

4 Dieticians are very different to nutritionists. _____

5 Dieticians sometimes do scientific research, nutritionists don't. _____

6 Dieticians earn a lot of money. _____

7 More men become nutritionists, more women become dieticians. _____

8 There are different degrees for dieticians and nutritionists. _____

DICTATION

8 [1.17] Listen and complete the sentences from Exercise 6.

1 Well, I'm interested in _____.

2 Most dieticians work in hospitals or health clinics, _____.

3 If you want the chance to do research, _____.

4 Well, at undergraduate degree level _____.

SPELLING: past participles

9 Correct the spelling of the words in bold.

1 I have **knewn** her for ages. _known_

2 You have **tooken** the book to the library. _____

3 He has **maide** a big mistake._____

4 She has **becom** the new Prime Minister. _____

5 It has **bean** a lovely day. _____

6 We have **spokan** to the boss. _____

7 You have **drunck** all the water. _____

8 They have **beginned** the exam already. _____

EXTRA VOCABULARY: health (illness and injury)

1 Use your dictionary. Put the words into the correct column.

| asthma   a black eye   ~~a broken leg~~ |
| a burnt hand   a bruised arm   a cold |
| a cough   a cut finger   diarrhoea   flu |
| a headache   ~~a high temperature~~   measles |
| a sore throat   a stomach-ache   a twisted ankle |

illness and symptoms	injuries
a high temperature	*a broken leg*

EXTRA LANGUAGE

We use *have got* to talk about illnesses and injuries.
  He's got a cold. I've got measles.
We use *hurt* and *ache* to talk about pain.
  My leg hurts. My right knee aches.
We use *hurt* if we have or cause an injury.
  I hurt my hands when I fell over.

2 Read the rules and complete the sentences with *have got, hurt* or *ache.*

1 David isn't at work today. He *has got* flu.

2 I _____ my head when I walked into the door.

3 What a long day at work! My head _____.

4 Many young children _____ asthma because of air pollution.

5 After walking today, my feet really _____.

6 I _____ my back when I slipped on the road.

PRONUNCIATION: intonation in *yes/no* questions

3a `1.18` Listen and complete the questions.

1 Do you often get *headaches?*

2 Have you ever been in _____?

3 Does your back still _____?

4 Have you done any exercise this _____?

5 Does he often take days off _____?

6 Do you ever get pains in your _____?

3b `1.18` Listen again and repeat the questions. Practise the correct intonation.

KEY LANGUAGE: giving advice and reasons

4 Give sensible advice to someone who wants to lose weight. Use the verbs in the box and *should* or *shouldn't.*

| ~~do~~   eat   put   run   see   stop |

1 He *should do* more exercise.

2 He _____ sugar in his coffee.

3 He _____ a marathon. It's too dangerous.

4 He _____ sitting in front of the TV all weekend.

5 He _____ a large meal late at night.

6 He _____ a doctor for more advice.

5 Complete these sentences with the words in the box.

| because   in order   so that   to |

1 She should change her job *because* she is unhappy at work.

2 _____ to save money, you shouldn't eat in restaurants.

3 You should join a sports club _____ meet more people.

4 You should buy a suit _____ you look smart at the interview.

5 _____ it is raining, you should cancel the day-trip.

1 Read the text. What type of word is missing from each space: a verb, a noun or an adjective?

1 _noun_   6 _____
2 _____   7 _____
3 _____   8 _____
4 _____   9 _____
5 _____

The history of medicine in Europe

The Chinese, Indian, Persian and Egyptian cultures developed early ideas of medicine, many years before similar ideas appeared in Europe. In 400 BC, Hippocrates wrote the first European ¹ _book_ about medicine. At this time, the focus was on diet and hygiene and there was very little knowledge of surgery and ² _____.

This approach to health care ³ _____ for over a thousand years until the work of people like Andreas van Wesel and William Harvey in the 1500s and 1600s. They examined bodies and started to ⁴ _____ experiments. This led to a better understanding of how the body works but it did not lead to many ⁵ _____ medicines or treatments. The ⁶ _____ change in European medicine came in the 1800s when chemistry and other sciences developed. ⁷ _____ such as Lister and Pasteur learnt how germs spread disease and how to make medicines. It was also the time when the ⁸ _____ work on genetics began with Mendel's experiments with peas. A hundred years later, Watson and Crick discovered DNA and Barnard ⁹ _____ the first heart transplant.

2 Complete the text with the words in the table.

nouns	verbs	adjectives
~~book~~	continued	big
medicine	do	early
scientists	performed	new

3 Match the sentences 1–5 with a–e.

1 Thanks for inviting me to the party.

2 Thank you for giving my phone number to Alice.

3 Thanks for lending me your lecture notes.

4 Thanks for sending me the Internet address.

5 Thank you for booking the tennis court.

a) They'll really help me with this essay. ___

b) You were right, it is a useful site. ___

c) She called me today. ___

d) I'm looking forward to our game. ___

e) I really enjoyed myself. _1_

4 Read the email. Replace the formal phrases in bold with these informal phrases.

Anyway	Bye for now	don't get	~~Hi, Tony~~
Guess what?	It's great	thanks again	
Thanks so much			

1 _Hi, Tony_   5 _____
2 _____   6 _____
3 _____   7 _____
4 _____   8 _____

¹**Dear Sir**

How are you? I'm very busy at the moment – my new job at the bookshop is certainly demanding. The shop opens late, so I ²**do not arrive** home until 9 p.m. most nights. But I'm so glad to have a job now. ³**I would like to thank you very much** for telling me about the job in the first place. I was desperate for work, and the bookshop is interesting. ⁴**I appreciate** working in the town centre, I can go to the shops at lunchtime – to spend some of my earnings! I met Richard the other day. ⁵**Have you heard his important news**? His wife's pregnant. Wonderful news.
⁶**I should finish the letter now**, hope to see you soon and ⁷**I would like to thank you once more** for your help.
⁸**Yours faithfully**
Sally

5 In your notebook write a short email to a friend. Tell them about something in your life at the moment (work, social life, hobbies, news).

5 Natural world

5.1 ISLANDS

VOCABULARY: landscapes

1 **Complete the words. Then answer the questions in your notebook.**

1 What's the highest m <u>o</u> <u>u</u> <u>n</u> t <u>a</u> <u>i</u> <u>n</u> in your country?

2 Have you ever walked along the top of a
c __ __ f __? When? Where?

3 Have you got a favourite b __ __ c __? Where is it? What colour is the sand?

4 Is there a r __ v __ __ in your capital city?

5 How far do you live from the c __ __ __ t?

6 What's the difference between a lake and a
l __ g __ __ __?

7 When was the first time you saw the s __ __?

8 Have you ever got lost in a f __ r __ __ t?

9 What's the name of the nearest h __ __ l to your house?

10 Which is more dangerous for ships, w __ v __ s or
r __ c __ s?

EXTRA VOCABULARY: landscapes

2 **Choose the correct word to complete these sentences.**

1 The ~~stream~~/dam/~~waterfall~~ was full because of all the rain.

2 The entrance to the scenery/caves/reservoirs was very narrow.

3 There were high valleys/dunes between the road and the shore/continents.

4 The Amazon is a jungle/wood/field in Brazil.

5 Please do not walk on the ground/grass/plain.

6 We left our boat at the bridge/lighthouse/jetty and had lunch at a fish restaurant.

SPELLING: geographical names

3 **1.19** **Listen and write the words.**

1 _Greenland_

2 _____

3 _____

4 _____

5 _____

6 _____

7 _____

8 _____

READING

4 **Read the descriptions and label the islands.**

| Sicily | Singapore | St Lucia |

1 _____

2 _____

3 _____

Singapore

Singapore is a small flat island country in South East Asia, off the coast of Malaysia. The weather is always hot and sticky. But Singapore isn't a typical tropical island, it's a rich, modern island city, with a population of nearly four and a half million. Most of the people are Chinese, and they live in the city at the southern end of the island. Singapore is the largest port in South East Asia, and the second largest in the world. It has a good education system and is clean and well-organised. It's a great place for shopping, too!

St Lucia (Note: we pronounce it: *Sint **Loo**sha*)

St Lucia is a small island country in the West Indies, to the east of the Caribbean Sea. It's a very green island, with mountains in the centre and beautiful sandy beaches around the coast. Like many Caribbean islands, it has a warm climate and it's famous for bananas. About 150,000 people live on the island, and most of them are Afro-Caribbean. The tourist industry is growing fast and this creates jobs for local people, especially in hotels and restaurants, but it also brings problems. Private companies are buying the land, and there is less room for small farms and local communities.

Sicily

Sicily lies between Europe and Africa, and it is the largest island in the Mediterranean Sea. There are large areas of mountains in the north and east. The highest point is Mount Etna (3,320 metres), which is the highest volcano in Europe. Sicily is extremely hot in summer, but in spring and autumn the climate is very pleasant. It is part of Italy, but it is quite independent. Five million people live there. Sicily has a long and complicated history and a rich culture. Fruit (lemons, grapes, etc) is one of the main products, but tourism is becoming more important. Sicily is also famous for the Mafia – an organisation of criminals.

READ BETTER: answering questions

When you answer questions about a text, identify the 'category' words in the questions. Then look for more 'specific' words in the text which match the category word. For example, specific words such as *room, kitchen, garden, garage* match the category word *house*.

5 Match the specific words in the box with the category words a) or b).

| field | island | mountain | snow | storm | wind |

a) weather _____

b) landscapes _____

6 Read the text again in Exercise 4. Name the island (or islands) which:

1 has different seasons *Sicily*

2 has a very small population _____

3 is near another country _____

4 has mountains _____

5 is between two continents _____

6 is never cold _____

7 is small _____

8 grows fruit _____

9 has a tourist industry that is developing

_____

10 is a country _____

GRAMMAR: prepositions

7 Complete the sentences with a preposition.

1 Bora Bora is surrounded *by* a lagoon.

2 Greenland is one _____ the most magical islands _____ the world.

3 Greenland lies _____ the North Atlantic and Arctic Oceans.

4 It's 2,655km _____ north _____ south.

5 Madagascar lies off the coast _____ Africa.

6 Many animals in Madagascar are _____ danger.

7 Great Britain is rich _____ history.

8 Trafalgar Square is _____ the heart _____ London.

GRAMMAR: comparatives and superlatives

8 Make sentences using the comparative or superlative form of the adjective.

1 Singapore / flat / of the three islands

Singapore is the flattest of the three islands.

2 Singapore / modern / of the three islands

_____

3 Singapore / good / place for shopping / St. Lucia

_____

4 history of Sicily / complicated / history of Singapore

_____

9 Make comparative or superlative sentences using *less … than*, and *the least*.

1 Sicily / green / St. Lucia

Sicily is less green than St. Lucia.

2 Sicily / tropical / of the three islands

_____

3 west of Sicily / hilly / north and east

_____

4 St Lucia / populated / Singapore

_____

VOCABULARY: animals

1 Find 12 animals in the wordsearch.

L	S	Q	U	I	R	R	E	L	T
H	E	H	U	M	A	N	L	E	Z
E	F	O	C	G	H	D	E	E	R
D	C	S	P	M	J	K	P	G	A
G	D	R	B	A	Y	B	H	I	B
E	Q	Y	A	E	R	E	A	R	B
H	W	U	K	B	X	D	N	A	I
O	S	N	A	I	L	R	T	F	T
G	O	R	I	L	L	A	L	F	A
M	H	U	O	P	T	I	G	E	R

GRAMMAR: expressions of quantity

2 Which of these sentences are grammatically incorrect? Find the mistakes and correct the sentences.

1 Nowadays, there are little water in Ethiopia.

   Nowadays, there is little water in Ethiopia.

2 There are very few panda bear in the world.

   _____

3 In Scotland, we killed many hedgehogs in the past to protect native birds.

   _____

4 There isn't many time to save the planet from humans.

   _____

5 Hedgehogs cause little damages to crops.

   _____

6 Do rabbits cause a lot problems?

   _____

7 Some animals cause many problems for farmers.

   _____

3 Complete this report about a plan for a new safari park in Congo. Use *much, many, a lot of, little* or *few*. Sometimes, more than one answer is possible.

New safari park in central Congo?

There are [1] *many/a lot of* reasons why this is a good area for the new park. I will cover the main ones here.

We don't need to worry about the local people because there are [2]_____ villages in the area. So, there is [3]_____ empty land that is usable. This land is good for [4]_____ different kinds of animal because there are [5]_____ rivers and [6]_____ jungle. This jungle will be good for the gorillas. The climate is good for our business – there isn't [7]_____ rain during the main tourist season. Fortunately, there are [8]_____ problems with the area. We only need to improve things for the tourists. For example, there is [9]_____ public transport in the region and there are [10]_____ roads. Also, we want to employ local people as guides but they don't speak [11]_____ English. There aren't [12]_____ other places for tourists to visit but this is not so important. Unfortunately, we have little time to improve these things. However, with [13]_____ hard work and if we spend [14]_____ money, I think we can open a successful safari park here in time for the tourist season.

TRANSLATION

4 Translate into your language. Notice the differences.

1 I've got a lot of homework this weekend.

   _____

2 There are few tall buildings in my town.

   _____

3 Is there much information in the brochure about the accommodation?

   _____

4 Have you got many things to do today?

   _____

5 There's little water in the lake because of the drought

   _____

Sometimes you only need to understand certain information or details. Before you listen, check what information you need. For example, in a listening exam, read the questions carefully before you listen, and check for key words.

- When listening, use key words to help you find the details you need.
- Do not worry about the information or details that you don't need.

5 Which of the key words would you listen for in these cases?

1 You want to know the cost of a concert.
   a) price   b) opening hours   c) ticket
   d) performers   e) discount

2 You want to find out about winter holiday deals in Canada.
   a) January   b) sailing   c) mountain
   d) accommodation and ski pass   e) beach

3 You want to find out about the weather at the weekend.
   a) forecast   b) Saturday   c) next week
   d) rainy   e) hot and dry

LISTENING

6 **1.20** Listen to the information about some holiday events and complete the table.

	Name of the event		Opening hours: days and times
1	Monkey Madness	1	
2		2	
3		3	

	Ticket prices		Transport
1	$2	1	
2		2	Small parking lot Train station near
3	$1 per talk /guided tour	3	

7 Answer these questions about the events in Exercise 6.

1 Which event is definitely indoors?
   Find the Facts

2 At which events don't you pay extra?
   _____

3 At which events can you touch living animals?
   _____

4 Which events take place in the city?
   _____

5 At which events do you find out about unusual animals?
   _____

6 Which event is only for children?
   _____

VOCABULARY: nouns and verbs

8 Complete the sentences with the words in the box. Use each word both as a noun *and* a verb.

cause   damage   hope   plant   ship

1 I travelled from New York to London by _ship_.
2 Everyone _____ that we can stop global warming.
3 There are some lovely _____ in this park.
4 Are we really _____ the extinction of tigers?
5 It takes weeks to _____ the goods from China.
6 Did you _____ your car in the accident?
7 We _____ the seeds after the rainy season.
8 I still have some _____ that my team can win.
9 What are the _____ of air pollution?
10 Do rabbits really _____ crops?

DICTATION

9 **1.21** Listen and complete this part of the radio broadcast in your notebook.

First of all, the zoo has an event for children called 'Monkey Madness'.

1 **Match the headings 1–5 with the sentences a–e.**

1 animal captivity

2 animal hospitals

3 illegal hunting

4 animal sanctuaries

5 animal rescue

a) We give wildlife a chance to live in safety, perhaps in a conservation park. ___

b) We work to improve the treatment of animals in zoos. _1_

c) Our experienced vets carry out hundreds of operations a day. ___

d) We save animals in emergency situations, perhaps after a ship sinks. ___

e) We train wildlife officers to stop the people who shoot wild animals. ___

KEY LANGUAGE: describing photographs

2 **Complete the descriptions of the photographs.**

1

In the first picture, we ¹ _can_ see a monkey in a zoo. The monkey is ²_____ a glass window. It is on the ³_____ of the picture. On the ⁴_____, there is a boy ⁵_____ is looking at the monkey. One person is ⁶_____ a photograph of the monkey.

2

The second picture ¹_____ some people who are rescuing a turtle on the beach. The turtle is on the ground in the middle ²_____ the picture. ³_____ are two people who are pulling the turtle. ⁴_____ the background there are a lot of people who are watching the rescue. The rescuers don't ⁵_____ very professional because they are wearing casual clothes.

3

In the third picture ¹_____ is a flood in a street. In the ²_____ of the picture there is a large dog ³_____ is sitting in a small boat. Next to the boat, on the ⁴_____, there is a man ⁵_____ is walking in the water and pulling the boat. In the ⁶_____, we can see some houses and another small boat.

PRONUNCIATION: weak forms and schwa

3a **Look at these sentences from Exercise 2. Underline the vowels with the schwa sound.**

1 In th<u>e</u> first pict<u>ure</u>, we <u>can</u> see <u>a</u> monkey in <u>a</u> zoo.

2 The second picture shows some people who are rescuing a turtle at the beach.

3 The turtle is on the ground in the middle of the picture.

4 Next to the boat, on the right, there's a man who is walking in the water.

5 In the background we can see some houses and another small boat.

3b **1.22** **Listen and check your answers.**

STUDY SKILLS: time management

1 Complete the advice with the verbs in the box.

take	decide	keep	be	make (x2)
organise	~~find~~			

1 *Find* out when you study best.

2 _____ what's important.

3 _____ a diary – and check it.

4 _____ regular breaks.

5 _____ lists of things you need to do.

6 _____ your files.

7 _____ sure you can concentrate.

8 _____ nice to yourself, find time to relax.

WRITING SKILLS: a comparative essay

2 Write pairs of contrastive sentences using the linking word in brackets.

1 Spider crabs are 30 cms wide.

Pea crabs are 0.5 cms wide.

a) Spider crabs *are 30cms wide, whereas pea crabs are only 0.5cms wide* (whereas)

b) Pea crabs *are 0.5cms wide. In contrast, Spider crabs are 30cms wide.* (in contrast)

2 Blue whales weigh about 150 tons.

Grey whales weigh about 50 tons.

a) Blue whales _____

_____ (whereas)

b) Grey whales _____

_____ (but)

3 Ostriches are 2.5m long.

Hummingbirds are 7cms long.

a) Ostriches _____

_____ (in contrast)

b) Hummingbirds _____

_____ (whereas)

4 Mayflies live for one day.

Giant tortoises live for over 100 years.

a) Mayflies _____

_____ (in contrast)

b) Giant tortoises _____

_____ (but)

3 Complete the text with the phrases a–f.

a) In contrast, the Red Sea is very hot

b) but it is very cold

c) it is only 55m deep

d) It is roughly 440,000km^2 in size

e) and it is also one of the hottest (28°C)

f) and there are many coral reefs

g) ~~They have also become major tourist destinations.~~

h) particularly for people on diving holidays

The world's seas are an important part of the global environment. They are home to thousands of species, they affect the weather and they provide food. [1] *g* This essay compares two seas in the northern hemisphere. The Baltic Sea, in Northern Europe, is part of the Atlantic Ocean. It is about 380,000km^2 in size and, on average, [2]____. This sea is not very salty (one percent) [3]____. Because of this, sea ice often covers nearly 50 percent of the surface. This means that there are not very many different animals that live in the sea.

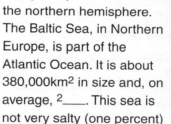

The Red Sea, between Africa and the Middle East, is part of the Indian Ocean. [4]____ and it has an average depth of 500m. This is one of the saltiest seas in the world (3.8 percent) [5]____. This warm environment is ideal for thousands of species [6]____ and tropical fish. This sea is very popular for tourists, [7]____.

To sum up, these two seas are similar in size but the Red Sea is deeper than the Baltic Sea. The Baltic Sea is a cold sea with a lot of ice. [8]____. The biggest difference concerns the biology of these seas. There are few species in the Baltic Sea, whereas there are many different species in the Red Sea. The warmer water also means that the Red Sea is a more popular tourist destination.

6 Society and family

6.1 FUTURE OPPORTUNITY

VOCABULARY: ages

1 Match the ages in the box with the definitions 1–8.

| 7 | 15 | 17 | ~~25~~ | 36 | 52 | 67 | 82 |

1 a young adult   _25_

2 a child   ——

3 an adolescent   ——

4 an elderly person   ——

5 a middle-aged person   ——

6 a teenager   ——

7 a retired person   ——

8 a thirty-something   ——

GRAMMAR: *will, might* and *may* for predictions

2 Put the words in the correct order.

1 There station Moon might a space on the be

There _might be a space station on the Moon._

2 We newspapers won't read the to get news definitely

We _____.

3 The might USA be not strongest the world's economy

The USA _____.

4 Brazil a will have strong probably economy

Brazil _____.

5 Families children than now will have fewer definitely

Families _____.

6 We probably drive use petrol won't cars that

We _____.

7 There cities may problems in be many our

There _____.

8 We definitely use the different Internet to do many things will

We _____.

9 The planet a lot hotter will global be because of warming

The planet _____

10 We won't hours in a week probably work fewer

We _____.

READ BETTER: predicting content

Use the title of a text, or the headline of an article, to predict the main contents of the text before you read it. Identify the general topic and think about the following questions.

- What do you know about this topic already?
- What vocabulary do you think will be in the text?
- What key points or argument do you think the text will make?

3 Match three phrases from the box with each headline.

| advanced technology   artificial intelligence |
| care homes   clubs and hobbies |
| ~~higher salaries~~   hospitals   longer holidays |
| later retirement   more unemployment |

1 **How lives will change as leisure time and incomes increase**

higher salaries, _____

2 **Big increase in the percentage of elderly people**

_____

3 **Robots: friend or enemy?**

_____

READING

4 Read the article headline. Make predictions about the content. Write down seven words you think you will see in the text. Then, read the text and check your predictions.

_____

_____

_____

5 Match the paragraphs A–E with the headings 1–5.

1 The old city, the new city _____A_____

2 A new style of life _____

3 Trees, plants and animals _____

4 Housing, offices and transport _____

5 Finance and demand _____

6 Are these statements true, false, or does the text not say?

1 In the future, the majority of the global population will live in urban areas. _true_

2 Power stations will supply green electricity for the buildings. _____

3 There will not be any cars in the city. _____

4 People won't live far from buses and trains. _____

5 Roofs will look like gardens. _____

6 The city will import food from the mainland. _____

7 It will be expensive to build this city. _____

8 Other countries are copying the Chinese ideas. _____

9 The green city won't be noisy. _____

China's urban future: greener and cleaner

A Cities are famously bad for the environment. They are heavy polluters. They cover the countryside with concrete. They make people stressed. By 2030, 60 percent of the world's population will live in cities. If cities stay the same, this will be an environmental disaster. However, some people in China are predicting a different future. By 2030, in Dontang, on Chongmin island near Shanghai, half a million people will live in a city that is good for the environment—one that is environmentally-friendly. They will live in a green city.

B The main changes will be in the urban areas. All the buildings in Dontang will produce their own electricity from solar and wind power. There will be no petrol cars, only electric ones, and all the homes will only be seven minutes away from public transport. There will be many canals in the city, and solar-powered water taxis will take people around the city.

C The planners have also thought about the green spaces. All residents will live near small parks and there will be grass and plants on the roofs of most buildings. There will be farms on the island that use organic methods. The plan is that this island city will produce all the food that it needs and that there will be large areas of open countryside.

D This project won't be cheap. It might cost £100 billion dollars. However, China needs to change the way its cities work. It already has over 90 cities with more than a million people, and this number will double in the next five years. There is no future for polluted and polluting cities.

E The green city will improve the quality of life for the residents. They will breathe clean air, they will live near their work place and they will live in a quiet city. Just imagine how quiet the city will be without petrol cars. Can you imagine?

LISTENING

THE NETHERLANDS (HOLLAND)
Amsterdam
Hook of Holland
Rotterdam

1 [1.23] **Listen to four people talking and choose the best summary.**

1 The Netherlands is a very free country and children there can do what they like. ____

2 The Netherlands is a good place to be a child because there is a good family environment. ____

3 A lot of people in the Netherlands work part-time, especially women. ____

4 Britain is the worst place in the developed world for children to grow up. ____

2 [1.23] **Listen again. Match the speakers a–d with the sentences 1–6.**

a) Female British TV presenter

b) Male British TV reporter

c) Male Dutch professor

d) Female Dutch professor

1 There are a lot of special play areas for children in the town. _b_

2 Fathers do a lot of activities with their children. ____

3 Parents want their children to enjoy themselves while they're growing up. ____

4 The UNICEF report looked at children in the 21 richest countries in the world. ____

5 Women often take a long break from their jobs when they have a child. ____

6 Children don't wear uniforms at school. ____

3 [1.24] **Listen to the next extract and complete the sentences. Use a maximum of three words.**

1 One reason for the Dutch success is the good _relationship between_ parents and children.

2 They can talk _____.

3 In the Netherlands, _____ of 15-year-olds eat the main meal of the day with their parents several times a week.

4 People can use that freedom and education to make _____.

5 At the same time, we give them the freedom to explore and to _____.

6 Dutch children have a _____ about themselves.

7 One problem is that children _____ what happens in the family!

SPELLING: vowels

4 **Some of these words have one incorrect letter. Correct the incorrect words.**

1 averege   _average_

2 birth rete   _____

3 childcare   _____

4 figure   _____

5 immidiate   _____

6 incourage   _____

7 percentige   _____

8 typicul   _____

VOCABULARY: negative adjectives

5 **Use the words in the box with *un-* or *-less* to complete the sentences.**

care	clear	comfortable	fair
fit	help	~~home~~	tidy

1 There are 50,000 _homeless_ children living on the streets of Addis Ababa, Ethiopia.

2 The instructions for the new TV are really _____. I can't understand anything at all.

3 He broke a lot of glasses when he was doing the washing-up – he's very _____.

4 Those children never do any exercise. They're very _____.

5 Humans are different to many other animals because they are _____ for a very long time after birth.

6 She's very _____ so her room is always a terrible mess.

7 All my friends from school can go on holiday with their families in August, but I can't – it's really _____.

8 The new dining-room chairs are really _____. My back aches.

DICTATION

6 **1.25** **Listen and write the sentences.**

1 _____

2 _____

3 _____

4 _____

GRAMMAR: first conditional

7 **Match phrases 1–6 with a–f to make first conditional sentences. Use *will* or *might*.**

1 ~~miss my next class~~

2 put on weight

3 rains this weekend

4 get home late tonight

5 computer crashes and I lose my work

6 there aren't any tickets for the football match

a) stay at home

b) go straight to bed

c) scream

d) go to the gym

e) watch it on TV

f) ~~find out what happened from other students~~

1 *If I miss my next class, I'll find out what happened from other students.*

2 _____
_____

3 _____
_____

4 _____
_____

5 _____
_____

6 _____
_____

PRONUNCIATION: *What'll*

8a **Your best friend wants to do a round-the-world trip. Use the words to ask her/him questions.**

1 What / if / your parents / not like / idea ?
What'll you do if your parents don't like the idea?

2 What / if / feel lonely ?
_____

3 What / if / be / ill ?
_____

4 What / if / run / money ?
_____

5 What / if / not speak / language ?
_____

8b **1.26** **Listen, repeat and check your answers.**

TRANSLATION

9 **Translate into your language. Notice the differences.**

1 My mother will be angry if I forget her birthday.
_____

2 What will you do if you lose your job?
_____

3 If they don't help me, I won't help them.
_____

4 What will happen if we don't arrive on time?
_____

5 Will you tell her the news if you see her?
_____

EXTRA VOCABULARY: members of the family

1 Choose the odd-one-out in each group.

1 brother, uncle, (sister,) son

2 husband, father, grandmother, brother-in-law

3 mother, mother-in-law, step-mother, sister-in-law

4 aunt, nephew, niece, wife

2 Match some of the words from Exercise 1 to these definitions.

1 Your sister's daughter   _niece_

2 Your father's second wife   _____

3 Your mother's mother   _____

4 Your father's or mother's sister   _____

5 Your mother's brother   _____

6 Your husband's mother   _____

7 Your sister's son   _____

8 Your husband's or wife's sister   _____

KEY LANGUAGE: expressing opinions

3a Complete the discussion with the words in the box.

completely	good	interesting	should (x2)
~~think~~	understand	what	with

TOM: The government has suggested that people with children should pay less tax. What do you ¹ _think_ of that?

BETH: Well, personally, I ² _____ disagree with that idea. It's their choice to have children, why should they pay less tax?

TOM: I ³ _____ your opinion, but we need to encourage people to have bigger families. I think the government ⁴ _____ reduce the tax for every child that a parent has.

JESS: I agree ⁵ _____ you. So, if you have three children you pay less tax than if you have one child.

DAN: Well, that's an ⁶ _____ idea, but don't forget that every new child means that the government actually needs more money, for schools and hospitals.

BETH: Exactly. ⁷ _____ I think is that parents should pay more tax, in order to cover the extra costs to society of a child.

JESS: That's a ⁸ _____ point, but then people won't have bigger families, and our country needs more young people.

TOM: Well, what ⁹ _____ we do then?

DAN: I'm not sure, but perhaps changes in tax aren't the answer.

3b ▣ 1.27 Listen and check your answers.

PRONUNCIATION: word linking (consonant to vowel)

4 ▣ 1.28 Listen and mark the links between words.

1 What do you **think‿of** that?

2 If you have three children you pay less tax than if you have one child.

3 Well, that's an interesting idea.

4 For schools and hospitals

5 In order to cover the extra costs

6 What I think is that

7 That's a good point.

8 And our country needs more young people.

STUDY SKILLS: correcting your writing

1 Correct the sentences. Either change the position of one word or add a new word.

1 My family is big quite. I've got three brothers.

My family is quite big. I've got three brothers.

2 We do a lot of things together; we go for often picnics.

_____

_____

3 I playing a computer game when my aunt called.

_____

4 We've got three pets; cat and two dogs.

_____

5 The CSA was a government department supported that families.

_____

_____

6 My mother has had a job ten years.

_____

2a Match the correction code symbols 1–6 with the meanings a–f.

1	WW		a)	missing word
2	SP		b)	grammar
3	MW		c)	punctuation
4	GR		d)	wrong word
5	WO		e)	spelling
6	P		f)	word order

2b Look at the correction codes and make the corrections.

1 My family is quite large for ~~the~~ *an* Austrian family.   WW

2 I have got two older brothers and a yuonger sister.   SP

3 My sister and I still live home with our parents,   MW

4 but my two older brothers leave home. They   GR

5 live both in Britain, the oldest one is in Scotland   WO

6 and the other one live in Wales.   GR

7 Both of my parents work. My father is chemist   MW

8 and, my mother is a teacher.   P

WRITING SKILLS: an article

3 Put the paragraphs in the correct order. Which country do you think the writer comes from?

1 _B_   2 ____   3 ____   4 ____

She comes from _____.

4 Choose the correct linkers to complete the article.

A Our national teams in athletics, swimming, rugby, cricket, hockey and netball have all been world champions. [1]*However/Because of* this, sport has made my country famous. Everyone in my country is proud of our sports players [2]*as/because of* they train hard to achieve wonderful results for us. Also, in 2000 we hosted the Olympic Games. We are one of only three countries that have sent athletes to every Olympic Games [3]*so/as* I can honestly say we are dedicated to global sport.

B There are many different things that I admire about my country [4]*because of/so* it is not easy to choose one thing that makes me proud. [5]*However/So*, there is one thing that seems the most important [6]*as/so* it has made my country famous all over the world. This thing is our love of sport.

C [7]*Because of/However* our love of sport I think my country has a great future. Sport keeps us strong and healthy which is important for a society. [8]*So/However*, sport is more than a physical skill. It also teaches us important values such as fairness, and [9]*so/because of* our society is more tolerant. I am proud of our love of sport [10]*however/because of* all these benefits that it brings to us.

D [11]*However/As*, I am not only proud of our international sporting success. I also love the way that everyone in my country takes part in sport. For example, at weekends, parks are full of people playing all kinds of sports. [12]*As/Because of* this I think we are friendly and sociable people – sport brings us all closer together.

PUNCTUATION

5 Correct the punctuation using capital letters, commas, apostrophes and full stops.

according to professor norbert schneider of mainz university the reasons for germanys low birth rate include poor childcare a school day that ends at 1pm and old-fashioned attitudes among employers

_____

_____

_____

_____

7 Science

7.1 CRIME LAB

VOCABULARY: words from the lesson

1 Which noun does <u>not</u> usually go with the verb?

1 to solve (an exam)/a problem/a crime

2 to discover *an idea/a clue/the truth*

3 to reveal *the truth/a secret/a drama*

4 to analyse *some evidence/a witness/a problem*

5 to commit *a crime/a secret/suicide*

6 to do *a decision/a test/some research*

7 to take *a picture/notes/research*

8 to interview *a witness/an application/a suspect*

2 Look at words and make nouns and verbs.

1 burgle (verb)

  a) *burglar* (noun, person)

  b) *burglary* (noun)

2 investigation (noun)

  a) _____ (noun, person)

  b) _____ (verb)

3 discoverer (noun, person)

  a) _____ (noun)

  b) _____ (verb)

4 examiner (noun, person)

  a) _____ (noun)

  b) _____ (verb)

5 analysis (noun)

  a) _____ (noun, person)

  b) _____ (verb)

GRAMMAR: *must* and *have to*

3 Correct the mistakes in these sentences.

1 You has to get a licence to drive a car.

  You have to get a licence to drive a car.

2 We must to finish the work by Friday.

  _____

3 I don't must forget to pay the phone bill.

  _____

4 They doesn't have to.

  _____

5 She must passes this exam.

  _____

6 What does he has to do today?

  _____

4 Complete the sentences about the UK with the correct form of *have to* or *must*.

1 At university …

  a) You *don't have to* wear a uniform.

  b) You _____ take exams.

  c) You _____ copy or plagiarise.

  d) You _____ go to every lecture.

2 In a library …

  a) You _____ turn off your phone.

  b) You _____ pay to borrow books.

  c) You _____ return books on time.

  d) You _____ smoke.

READ BETTER: text organisation

Before you read a text, you can predict some of the possible content or information. You can also predict in what order the information will appear.

• Think about how we organise common types of text, (e.g. articles, stories) before you read.

5 Look at this newspaper headline and predict the order of the information a–e.

New invention will save millions of lives

a) Possible disadvantages of the invention

b) ~~Summary of what the invention is and what it does~~

c) Details about how the invention works

d) Who did the research and where

e) The future development plans for the invention

1 *b*   2 ___   3 ___   4 ___   5 ___

READING

6 Before you read the text about the history of the microscope, predict the order in which the information a–e will appear. Read the text quickly to check your answers.

a) The invention of the microscope

b) The discovery of glass and early lenses

c) Definition of a microscope

d) Modern microscopes

e) Later developments and improvements

f) The pioneers – early users of the microscope

1 _c_   2 ___   3 ___   4 ___   5 ___   6 ___

History of the microscope

A microscope is a scientific instrument that reveals objects which are normally too small for the human eye to see. Microscopes use several lenses to provide a large image of a tiny object and they have been
5 important in the study of Biology.

The discovery of glass over 2000 years ago led to early experiments with lenses. People noticed that single lenses could make objects larger and also that they could focus the sun's rays to start a fire. These early
10 lenses were called 'burning glasses'. This led to the development of eye-glasses or spectacles in the early 1300s.

In the late 1500s, two Dutch spectacle makers, Hans and Zaccharias Janssen, invented the first true
15 microscope. They used several lenses together in a tube and discovered that they could make objects look many times bigger. Galileo, an Italian scientist, improved the quality of the lenses to produce better quality microscopes and telescopes.

20 Anthony Leeuwenhoek (1632–1723) and Robert Hooke (1635–1703) were two early users of the microscope who made many important
25 discoveries. Leeuwenhoek discovered bacteria and showed how a drop of water is full of living creatures. Robert Hooke wrote a book *Micrographia*
30 which described this new world of micro-organisms, with drawings that amazed the world.

For two hundred years, there was little development of the microscope until new industrial techniques

produced accurate and powerful lenses. Before this 35 time, people made the lenses by hand and they were often inaccurate. In the early twentieth century, the USA and Germany produced powerful microscopes (x1000) in large 40 numbers for export around the world.

Nowadays, scientists still use microscopes that use light to see small objects such as cells and 45 micro-organisms. However, they also have extremely powerful microscopes that use a different technology. These electron microscopes have a magnification of a million times and now we can see 50 molecules and atoms.

7 Answer these questions in your notebook.

1 What do microscopes show us?

They show us things which are normally too small for the human eye to see.

2 Which science has used microscopes a lot?

3 Why were early lenses called 'burning glasses'?

4 When did people first use lenses to improve their eyesight?

5 How did Galileo make better quality microscopes?

6 What was the name of Robert Hooke's book?

7 What was the problem with hand-made lenses?

8 Which countries became major industrial producers of microscopes?

9 What type of microscope lets us see the smallest things in the world?

8 Find these words in the text. What do they refer to?

1 which (line 2) _____

2 they (line 4) _____

3 they (line 8) _____

4 This (line 10) _____

5 They (line 15) _____

6 who (line 24) _____

7 which (line 30) _____

8 this time (line 35-36) _____

9 that (line 44) _____

10 they (line 46) _____

VOCABULARY: science

1 Complete the definitions of these subjects with words from the box.

business	chemicals	combine
illnesses	injuries	in the past
living things	money	movement
numbers	~~planets~~	~~stars~~

1 Astronomy — the study of _stars_ and _planets_

2 Biology — the study of _____

3 Chemistry — the study of _____ and what happens to them when they change or _____ with each other

4 Economics — the study of _____ and _____

5 History — the study of things _____

6 Mathematics — the study of _____

7 Medicine — the study of _____ and _____

8 Physics — the study of heat, light, sound and _____ .

VOCABULARY: nouns, adjectives and verbs with prepositions

2 Choose the correct prepositions to complete the sentences.

1 She's wasn't interested *in/of/at* Chemistry at school.

2 I have a good relationship *of/for/with* my boss.

3 I'm afraid *to/of/by* snakes.

4 They're proud *of/with/in* their country.

5 Look at him! What's happened *at/to/with* him?

6 I spend all my money *to/on/in* computers.

7 They belong *at/for/to* the college boat club.

8 They received their prizes *from/by/of* the Prime Minister.

9 Her last book was about the history *of/in/for* science.

10 Thanks *to/at/for* you, I understand the homework.

SPELLING: difficult words

3 `1.29` Listen to the sentences and the word that is repeated. Write the repeated word.

1 _January_   5 _____

2 _____   6 _____

3 _____   7 _____

4 _____   8 _____

LISTENING

4a `2.2` Listen to the conversation between Kevin and Jane and choose the best answers a), b) or c).

1 Kevin and Jane are probably …

   a) students in their first year of undergraduate study

   b) graduate research students

   c) young university lecturers at the start of their career

2 What is the main topic of their conversation?

   a) Stephen Hawking's work

   b) Hawking's character

   c) the duties of the job of Hawking's assistant

THE RECORD-BREAKING BESTSELLER NOW IN PAPER

A BRIEF HISTORY OF TIME
From the Big Bang to Black Holes

'This book marries a child's wonder to a genius's intellect. We journey into Hawking's universe, while marvelling at his mind'
Sunday Times

Introduction by Carl Sagan

STEPHEN HAWKING

4b [2.2] **Listen again. Complete the notes about what Hawking's assistant has to do. Use a maximum of three words.**

1 do _the shopping_

2 help prepare his lectures and _____

3 travel all _____ with him

4 book hotels _____

5 _____ to conferences

6 stand on stage with him _____

7 answer _____

4c [2.2] **Listen again and tick the words you hear about Stephen Hawking.**

1 amazing   ____

2 brilliant   ✓

3 calm   ____

4 determined   ____

5 different   ____

6 disappointed   ____

7 exciting   ____

8 frightening   ____

9 hard   ____

10 inspiring   ____

11 interesting   ____

12 strange   ____

TRANSLATION

5a **Translate into your language. Note the differences.**

1 Most people don't know much about science.

_____

2 Because of their knowledge, scientists have a power that makes them dangerous.

_____

3 TV programmes about science are boring.

_____

4 I think experiments on animals are wrong.

_____

5b **Do you agree with the statements in Exercise 5a? Write your answers and explanations.**

1 _____
_____

2 _____
_____

3 _____
_____

4 _____
_____

GRAMMAR: _had to_ and _could_

6 **Read the sentences and write sentences that mean the same. Use the correct form of _had to_ and _could_.**

1 It was necessary for her to work all night to finish the report.

She had to work all night to finish the report.

2 They weren't able to escape.

_____

3 Was he able to play the piano when he was five?

_____

4 Was it necessary for you to write a lot of essays last year?

_____

5 Everyone at the conference spoke some English so we were able to communicate.

_____

6 It wasn't necessary for me to have an operation.

_____

DICTATION

7 [2.3] **Listen and write the conversation.**

ROB: _____

_____

LUCY: _____

_____

ROB: _____

_____

LUCY: _____

_____

VOCABULARY: science facts

1 Complete the sentences with the words in the box.

> electricity   genetics   infinity   levers and pulleys
> molecules   printing press   psychoanalysis
> refrigerators   ~~theory of relativity~~   vaccination

1 Einstein published his *theory of relativity* in 1905.

2 In 460BC, the Greek philosopher Leucippus proposed the existence of atoms and

_____ .

3 In 400BC, Indian mathematicians wrote about the concept of _____ .

4 The discovery of the structure of DNA in 1953 led to great advances in _____ .

5 Edward Jenner and Louis Pasteur were pioneers of _____ techniques.

6 Guttenberg, of Germany, invented the _____ in 1445.

7 Sigmund Freud was the founder of _____ .

8 The Greek philosopher Archimedes (287–212BC) is famous for his engineering inventions that used

_____ .

9 In 1750, the American scientist Benjamin Franklin showed that lightning is _____ .

10 People first used _____ in their kitchens at home in the 1920s.

PRONUNCIATION: voiced and unvoiced consonants

2a Identify the phonemic sounds in each word. Write which sounds are voiced (V) or unvoiced (UV).

Unvoiced	/p/	/t/	/k/	/f/	/θ/	/s/	/ʃ/	/tʃ/
Voiced	/b/	/d/	/g/	/v/	/ð/	/z/	/ʒ/	/dʒ/

pack	/p/ UV	back	/b/ V
town		down	
good		could	
safe		save	
think		those	
raise		race	
pleasure		pressure	
joking		choking	

2b 2.4 Listen and check your answers.

KEY LANGUAGE: developing an argument

3a Choose the best phrases to complete the text.

The most important invention of the twentieth century

The invention that I think is the most important is the Internet. It [1]*has led to / means* great changes in our lives, particularly in the areas of communication, information, creativity and business.

First of all, email [2]*caused / means* that we can communicate very quickly, efficiently and cheaply. This [3]*is connected to / so* the globalisation of business because doing business is now much easier and quicker. It has also [4]*led to / caused* people having personal relationships across the world. We can see this in the multinational chat rooms.

Secondly, the Internet is a great library of information. This [5]*means / is connected to* that people do not depend on the few hundred books in their local library, instead they can read billions of documents and files. People can find out about history, entertainment and their holiday destinations at the click of a button.

Thirdly, the Internet [6]*has led to / so* the development of a new type of business: e-business. Nowadays, a business does not need to have a building, and [7]*so / means* it is easier and cheaper to start a business. Also, on an individual level, it is very convenient for the customers who can now shop from their home.

Finally, the Internet [8]*has caused / meant that* a great increase in creativity. For example, people put videos online, they write blogs or start their own websites. This shows that the Internet [9]*means that / has led to* positive or active changes in people's lives, whereas inventions like the television are less positive and more passive.

3b 2.5 Listen and check your answers.

STUDY SKILLS: making notes

1 Read the essay title. Compare the notes for the essay with the original text in Exercise 3. Find the missing information, mistakes and the irrelevant material in the notes.

How has the Internet changed the personal lives of individuals all over the world?

<u>Internet and individual, personal lives</u>

Internet → changes in 1) communication
2) entertainment 3) business 4) creativity

1   communication
    Email → quick, efficient communication
    a) business is easier and so it is more global
    b) personal relationships all over the world …

2   information
    large library of information
    a) millions of files → people can research any topic easily
    b) (history, … and …)

3   business
    1-business
    a) cheap to start a business
    b) inconvenient for individual customers – shop from home

4   creativity
    small increase
    a) personal videos, blogs and …
    b) negative/active changes (TV less positive)

WRITING SKILLS: describing charts

2 Look at the chart and complete these sentences.

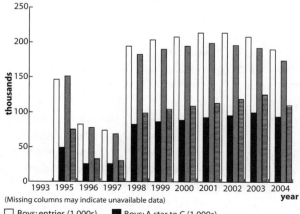

thousands / year

(Missing columns may indicate unavailable data)

☐ Boys: entries (1,000s)   ■ Boys: A star to C (1,000s)
▨ Girls: entries (1,000s)   ▤ Girls: A star to C (1,000s)

1 The white bar shows *the number of boys who took the GCSE exam in Design & Technology*.

2 The grey bar shows _____ _____ .

3 The black bar shows _____ _____ .

4 The striped bar shows _____ _____ .

3 Look at the chart and complete the text with a word or number.

This chart shows the [1] <u>number</u> of boys and girls who took the GCSE exam in Design & [2]_____ between 1995 and [3]_____ , and how many of them passed the exam with the highest grades, A star to C. In general, between 1995 and 2004 more [4]_____ than [5]_____ took the GCSE exam in Design & Technology. In contrast, more [6]_____ passed with grades A star to C than [7]_____ . In 1995 only, there were more [8]_____ than [9]_____ who took the exam.

4 Choose the correct words to complete the text.

Looking at the chart in more detail we can see that, in 1996, the number of boys and girls who took the exam [1]~~a fall~~ / *fell*. In 1995, 150,000 girls took the exam. In 1996, this number [2]*a decrease / decreased* to 75,000. There was [3]*a fall / fell* in the number of boys who took the exam from 145,000 to 80,000. In contrast, in 1998 there was [4]*an increase / increased* in the number of boys and girls who took the exam. In 1997, 75,000 boys took the exam. In 1998, this number [5]*an increase / increased* to 200,000. The number of girls [6]*a rise / rose* from 70,000 to 175,000. These numbers [7]*increased / increase* slowly until 2002.

5 Complete the next sentence in the description.

Between 2002 and 2004, the number of boys who took the exam _____ and there _____ _____ _____ _____ _____ .

6 Write a final paragraph of the description in your notebook. Describe what happened to the boys and girls who passed the exam with grades A–C.

8 The night

8.1 SLEEP TIGHT!

VOCABULARY: sleep

1a Complete the phrases with the verbs in the box.

be	fall	~~feel~~	go to	have	sleep
talk	wake				

1 to _feel_ sleepy

2 to _____ sleep

3 to _____ dreams / a good night's sleep / a sleepless night

4 to _____ sleepy / asleep

5 to _____ up

6 to _____ in / well / through the noise

7 to _____ into a deep sleep / asleep

8 to _____ in your sleep

READING

2a Complete the article with the correct words.

1b Now complete these sentences with some of the expressions from Exercise 1a.

1 There was a big storm last night. How did you _sleep through_ all the noise?

2 I usually _____ very early in the morning.

3 When he got home from work, his children _____ already _____ .

4 I didn't _____ last night, so I _____ sleepy now.

Why does it seem to be so difficult for teenagers to get up in the morning? Do they go to bed too late? Are [1] _they_ lazy? Or is there another reason beyond their control?

A growing body of evidence from sleep researchers suggests that young people need to sleep a lot. Mary Carskadon, a researcher in the biology of sleep, has shown that teenagers in [2] _____ USA sleep an average of seven and a half hours a night during the week. However, 25 percent only sleep six [3] _____ a half hours a night. To be fully awake, so that they can perform well, teenagers need about nine hours of sleep. Carskadon's work shows that the popular belief that children need [4] _____ sleep as they develop into young adults is false.

New research also shows that getting up in the morning really [5] _____ a big problem for young people. Tim Roenneberg and his team at the University of Munich have shown that sleep times change as we become older. In our early teens, bed times and wake times move to later and later hours. This pattern continues [6] _____ about the age of 19.5 years for women and 20.9 years for men. After this, the situation changes and young people start to have earlier bed and wake times. Roenneberg believes that this is [7] _____ effect of biology and not an effect of society.

Another problem for young people is that there is a Western cultural belief that we should [8] _____ active in the morning. We say, for example, 'early to bed, early to rise, makes a man healthy, wealthy and wise' and 'the early bird catches the worm.' However, this ignores the scientific evidence. Children and adults prefer mornings, [9] _____ teenagers and young adults prefer afternoons or evenings for both academic and physical activities.

The timetable of school and college life in many countries does not take into account the sleep problems that teenagers face. So what's the conclusion? Well, a later starting time for school and college would improve the mental ability and performance of students [10] _____ their morning lessons. Perhaps we should think about starting lessons at 10.00 or 11.00 a.m., if we want our young people to be smart.

2b Answer these questions.

Who …

1 works at the University of Munich?

Tim Ronneberg and his team.

2 prefers mornings?

_____

3 is a researcher in the biology of sleep?

_____

4 starts to have earlier bed and wake times between the ages of 19 and 20?

_____

5 discovered that the time we go to bed and wake up changes during our lives?

_____

6 studied how long teenagers sleep in the USA?

_____

7 studied something that many people believe – and found that it was not true?

_____

8 believes that biology is the key element in understanding bed and wake times?

_____

9 believes that we should be active in the morning?

_____

GRAMMAR: verb patterns

3 Read this email from a university lecturer to his Head of Department. Then complete the replies with the correct form of the verbs.

To:	m.giacobelli@cpu.sa
From:	b.hall@cpu.sa
Subject:	class hours

Dear Mario,
Most of our classes currently start at 9.00 a.m.
I believe that if we start at 10.00 a.m. and have more classes in the afternoon, students will perform better and get better exam results.
I hope we can discuss this matter soon.
Regards
Brian

1 You seem _to be_ (be) really worried about the timetable.

2 Why did you decide _____ (raise) this question now?

3 I need _____ (think) about it more.

4 Keep _____ (look for) more research on this topic.

5 I want _____ (discuss) this issue with my bosses.

6 What are you hoping _____ (achieve)?

7 Have you thought about _____ (make) your nine o'clock classes more interesting?

8 You tend _____ (blame) the system.

9 I'm starting _____ (get) angry.

10 Do you like _____ (work) here?

4 Choose the correct word to complete the sentences.

1 I've always *dreamt/expected/wished* of living in a hot country.

2 She *complains/feels/appears* to be very unhappy in her new job.

3 He *worried/apologised/forgot* for arriving late.

4 They *succeeded/attempted/insisted* on paying for the meal.

5 They're *talking/concentrating/interested* about going to Cuba for their next holiday.

TRANSLATION

5 Translate into your language. Note the differences.

1 They'll enjoy listening to his talk.

_____

2 He succeeded in keeping the attention of the audience.

_____

3 I hate being late for class.

_____

4 I finally managed to fall asleep at 3.00 a.m.

_____

SPELLING: silent letters

6 These letters are sometimes silent: *b, c, g, h, k, l, n, s, t, w*. Underline the silent letters in these words.

1	answer	5	exhibition	9	know
2	autumn	6	half	10	listen
3	write	7	hour	11	science
4	doubt	8	island	12	sign

VOCABULARY: -ing/-ed adjectives

1 **Choose the correct adjectives to complete the sentences.**

1 Did you see that *fascinating/fascinated* documentary about wild bears last night?

2 I'm not *frightening/frightened* of ghosts, but then, I've never seen one.

3 I feel really *tiring/tired* today. I didn't sleep well last night.

4 My daughter was really *exciting/excited* when we gave her a bike.

5 He won't play chess. He thinks it's a *boring/bored* game.

6 I don't like dangerous sports. They're *frightening/frightened*.

7 I thought the Egyptian pyramids were *amazing/amazed*. How did they build them?

8 The football match was *exciting/excited*. The final score was 4:3.

9 She was *surprising/surprised* when she won the book prize. She didn't expect to win.

10 It's *embarrassing/embarrassed* when you forget people's names.

GRAMMAR: future intentions

2 **Put the words in the correct order to make sentences and questions.**

1 city a I would live like to in not

I would not like to live in a city.

2 is next month going start She a new job to

_____

3 she her new job hoping to What is achieve in ?

_____

4 they to their like to return country Would soon ?

_____

5 hoping Is sell she to her business day one ?

_____

6 What going weekend are to do you this ?

_____

3 **Choose the correct verb forms to complete the sentences.**

1 They *would like / are going* to get married next year, but they need to save some money first.

2 I'm afraid we definitely can't come to your party, we are *hoping / going* to visit my parents that weekend.

3 He *would like / is going* to leave his job, but he can't because he needs the money.

4 Which university are you *going / hoping* to go to? Have you had an interview yet?

5 I can give you a lift to work next week because *I'm going / I would like* to buy a car tomorrow.

LISTEN BETTER: signposts

When someone prepares a talk or presentation, they organise their ideas in sequence. When they give the talk, they use language to show this organisation, e.g. *Firstly, secondly, thirdly*, etc.

- This language is known as signpost language because it helps the listener to follow the direction of the talk.
- Listen carefully for signpost language.

4 **Put these signpost phrases in the order we normally hear them.**

a) Let's start by looking at … ____

b) Today I'm going to talk about … _1_

c) To conclude / To sum up … ____

d) Now, let's move on to … ____

LISTENING

5 **2.6** **Listen to a talk about the Moon. In what order does the lecturer discuss these points?**

a) The Moon and crime ____

b) The Moon and food ____

c) The shape and colour of the Moon _1_

d) The Moon and accidents ____

e) The Moon and our health ____

6 `2.6` **Listen again and answer these questions.**

1 What can we see at the time of the full moon?
A bright white circle.

2 What colour is the Moon?

_____

3 What does the Moon cause in our seas?

_____

4 By what percentage does the number of people visiting their doctor increase during the full moon?

_____

5 When does more crime happen?

_____

6 When does the largest number of car accidents happen?

_____

7 How much more food do we eat during a full moon?

_____

8 How many people have been to the Moon?

_____

DICTATION

7 `2.7` **Listen and complete the text.**

Hello _____

_____

_____

_____

_____

_____

_____

_____

PUNCTUATION

8 Correct the punctuation in these sentences, using capital letters, commas, apostrophes and full stops. There are two sentences.

when i came to this country the only work i could find was as a night security guard this job is boring because it is so quiet but ive decided to turn this problem into an advantage

_____

_____

_____

_____

1 Match the leisure activities with the correct verb expression.

> boat trip   cinema   dancing   dinner
> fireworks display   ~~museum~~   music concert
> sports event   theatre

1 go to a _museum_ / _____ / _____ /_____

2 go _____

3 go to the _____ / _____

4 go out for _____

5 go on a _____

PRONUNCIATION:
intonation in *Wh*- questions

2a Put the words in the correct order to make questions.

1 do would to What you like ?

What would you like to do?

2 to Where would like go you ?

_____

3 prefer What would do you to ?

_____

4 do What you would rather ?

_____

5 doing fancy you What do ?

_____

6 want What do to do you ?

_____

7 shall we do What dinner after ?

_____

8 on What's o'clock at about eight ?

_____

2b 〔2.8〕 Listen and check your answers. Repeat each question with the correct intonation.

3 Choose the correct verb forms to complete the phrases.

1 I'd love ~~being~~ / *to be* the first person.

2 I'm not keen *on going* / *on go* to the Eiffel Tower,

3 I'd *prefer not* / *not prefer* to visit a museum,

4 I don't mind *to do* / *doing* that.

5 I'd rather *go* / *going* for a walk than stay in bed.

6 I'd like *staying* / *to stay* in bed.

4a Hank, Joey and Tilly are from New York. They're visiting Paris for a long weekend. Complete the conversation with the sentences from Exercise 3.

HANK: Right then guys, let's sort our schedule. We get there Thursday evening, so, what shall we do Friday morning?

TILLY: ¹ 6

JOEY: Stay in bed! What do you mean? We haven't got time to stay in bed.

TILLY: I know, but I'll be tired. ²_____ or a gallery or anything like that.

HANK: Well, why don't we go for a nice walk by the River Seine?

JOEY: OK, that sounds good. ³_____ . Perhaps we can find a nice place for a late breakfast. Tilly?

TILLY: Sure, that sounds fine. And, shall we go to the Eiffel Tower in the afternoon?

JOEY: Yes, ⁴_____ . The view should be fantastic from there.

HANK: Oh, I don't know. ⁵_____ in the afternoon.

TILLY: Really? Why not?

HANK: Well, I think it'll be very busy. We should go early in the morning when it's quiet.

TILLY: Yeah, good idea. ⁶_____ to go up the tower. What shall we do in the afternoon?

JOEY: We could go and see some modern art at the Pompidou Centre?

HANK: Great idea! That's decided then.

4b 〔2.9〕 Listen and check your answers.

---

1 Complete the advice about improving your memory with the phrases in the box.

> the rooms in a large house   to make a story
> to remember them   read this book
> organising words into groups
> the skill of association
> ~~spend time memorising words~~   good vocabulary
> organise these lists alphabetically

One of the most important things to do when learning a language is to ¹ *spend time memorising words.* You might have good grammar, you might have good pronunciation, but without ²_____ you will find it hard to communicate. There are several ways you can remember words. The most basic way is to write them in a list in a vocabulary book. You could ³_____ . Then, you should regularly ⁴_____ and test your memory of the words. You can improve this technique by ⁵_____ . For example, you could group words by topic or by their grammar (noun, verb, adjective). Another useful strategy is to use ⁶_____ . This involves making connections between the new words and something else, for example ⁷_____ . This approach is all about creating a mental picture to help you remember the words. You can also use new words ⁸_____ . The important thing is that the words are not left on their own, they are connected to something else which helps you ⁹_____ .

WRITING SKILLS:
a story

2 Read the story. What kind of story is it?

1 A love story   ____

2 A horror story   ____

3 A crime story   ____

4 A ghost story   ____

3 Choose the correct linkers to complete the story.

I make nature documentaries for TV and this job can take you to some really wild places. About ten years ¹*ago/while*, I was working on a film about wild bears in the Black Mountains.

One ²*moment/night* I couldn't find my way back to my car. I walked round and round but I was completely lost. After some ³*time/while,* I saw an old tower at the top of a hill. The door was open so I went in and climbed the stairs. No-one seemed to live there. There was a room at the top which was quite clean and dry, so I decided to spend the night there.

It was still dark ⁴*finally/when* I woke up. I could hear a noise – a kind of click, click, click. ⁵*Suddenly/While* something white – like a ghost – appeared in the darkness and rushed towards me. I screamed in terror and ran down the stairs as fast as I could, leaving all my money and equipment behind.

After a ⁶*time/while*, I came to an open space and stopped running. At ⁷*last/finally*, I felt safe, but then, at that ⁸*suddenly/moment*, the ground started shaking under my feet. I ⁹*soon/long* realised it was an earthquake. I looked back. The tower at the top of the hill was leaning to one side. ¹⁰*When/Suddenly*, it fell down with a great crash. Before ¹¹*long/time*, the dust and smoke cleared and I could see that the tower was now just a pile of rocks and bricks. As I looked, I could see a white shape floating through the air.

Finally, _____ .

4 Complete the final paragraph of the story.

_____

_____

_____

_____

_____

_____

_____

_____

Work and industry

9.1 EMPLOYMENT

VOCABULARY: work

1 Tick the words and phrases that refer to a person or people.

1	colleague	✓	6 skills	___
2	employee	___	7 staff	___
3	manager	___	8 survey	___
4	opportunity	___	9 team	___
5	report	___	10 working conditions	___

2 Which of these things do you prefer in a job? Choose *one* option in each sentence.

1 having long lunch breaks OR doing training courses

_____

2 working long hours but getting good pay OR working shorter hours but getting less pay

_____

3 getting a payment for long service OR having a lot of staff parties

_____

4 running your own department in a small company OR working for a large market leader

_____

EXTRA VOCABULARY: nouns ending in –*tion*

3a Make nouns from these verbs using -*tion*. Mark the word stress on the nouns.

1	imagine	*imaginátion*
2	promote	_____
3	communicate	_____
4	direct	_____
5	educate	_____
6	inform	_____
7	invite	_____
8	operate	_____
9	organise	_____
10	present	_____

3b [2.10] Listen and check your answers.

READ BETTER: reading faster

To help you read faster, try these things:
- Don't follow the words with your pen. Just read using your eyes!
- Don't underline anything (e.g. words you don't know).

4 Read the article quickly. What is the main point?

1 to explain the differences between self-employed people in the UK and the USA

2 to show the differences between working for yourself and working for others

3 to describe the results of a survey by Professor Simon Parker

READING

5 Complete the text with the words in the box.

~~colleagues~~	decided	employees	full time
holidays	husband	levels	manage
spend	uncertain	valuable	women

6 Put these statements in the order that they appear in the text.

a) the number of people in Britain who are self-employed ___

b) Annette Fishburn's previous job ___

c) where Professor Simon Parker works *1*

d) the reasons why self-employed people work long hours ___

e) what Annette Fishburn wants to do in the future ___

f) which groups of people Professor Parker studied ___

g) working hours for employed and self-employed men ___

h) the name of Annette Fishburn's new company and what it does ___

i) working hours for employed and self-employed women ___

Time for a change?

Are you tired of travelling to the office every day? Are you bored with your [1] _colleagues_ ? Do you hate your boss? Then perhaps working for yourself is the answer.

Professor Simon Parker from Durham University looked at information about both employed and self-employed people in the UK and the USA in the 1990s. He found that people who run their own businesses enjoy high [2]_____ of job satisfaction. This is because of the flexibility and independence that working for themselves gives them. The ability to organise their own working hours is more [3]_____ to them than earning a lot of money. However, they usually work longer hours than employees. The survey showed that, on average, self-employed men work between 54 and 56 hours a week. Male [4]_____ . work about 44 hours.

[5]_____ who run their own businesses work about 17 hours a week more than female employees. Self-employed women work 47 hours a week, while female employees work about 30. Professor Parker said that people who run their own businesses worked longer hours because their financial situation is more [6]_____ .

About one in ten people in Britain is now self-employed. Annette Fishburn used to earn £40,000 a year when she had a [7]_____ job. She used to run training courses for small businesses. A year ago, she [8]_____ to become self-employed and started her own travel business. Her company, _Spirit Lifestyle_ organises [9]_____ to Umbria in Italy. She now pays herself £25,000 a year. She sometimes works 100 hours a week, but she insists that it's worth it. 'Although some days I work for 16 hours, other days I can go and meet a friend for coffee or go shopping.' She says that she is able to [10]_____ her own time to suit her, and this flexibility means more to her than money.

At first, it was hard, but things have gone well. Mrs Fishburn now has more time with her [11]_____ Andrew, 44. The couple, who have no children, plan to [12]_____ more time abroad – thanks to the business. 'My friends think I'm mad to work these hours,' she says. 'But I love my job.'

GRAMMAR: _used to_

7a Complete the sentences about a famous actress with _used to, didn't use to_ or _did ... use to_.

Before she was famous …

1 She _used to_ earn very little money.

2 _____ ride an old bike?

3 She _____ go to tropical islands for her holidays.

4 She _____ stay in five-star hotels.

5 She _____ travel first class on planes.

6 She _____ live in a small house.

7 _____ share a bedroom with her sister?

8 She _____ eat in cheap restaurants.

7b Complete the sentences with the correct form of _used to_ and one of the verbs in the box.

| be | ~~go~~ | laugh | listen | play | sleep |

1 For years, she _used to go_ to the gym every day.

2 _____ in the street a lot when you were a child?

3 My dad _____ to classical music when he was younger, but now he loves it!

4 Until she was 17, she _____ about ten hours a night.

5 There _____ a cinema on the corner, but they knocked it down.

6 He's very serious these days. _____ more when he was younger?

PRONUNCIATION: /s/ or /z/

8a Decide if we pronounce these words with /s/ or /z/. Then write them in the correct column.

~~because~~ ~~course~~ interested least skill small organisation pleasant research result enthusiastic survey to use used to years service works

/s/	/z/
course	because

8b [2.11] Listen and check your answers.

VOCABULARY: compound nouns

1 Complete these compound nouns.

1 sports ce*ntre*
2 postma*n*
3 car pa_____
4 airli_____
5 video sh_____
6 language tea_____
7 credit ca_____
8 sea be_____

9 webpa_____
10 newspa_____
11 lampsh_____
12 pop gr_____
13 shellfi_____
14 textbo_____
15 shopke_____

EXTRA VOCABULARY: gold

2 Choose ten things that are sometimes made of gold, or have gold in or on them.

(bathroom)   builder   car   computer
credit card   electricity   glass   jewellery
oil   pencil   plate   plastic   roof   silver
tooth

DICTATION

3 `2.12` **Listen and complete the text about the California Gold Rush in your notebook.**

In 1848, thousands of people rushed to California when someone found gold in the Sacramento River.

LISTEN BETTER: staying cool

Sometimes, the information you hear can be difficult to understand. Don't panic! If you become very nervous, you won't understand anything.

• Try to relax. Breath slowly and stay calm, but continue to concentrate. You might find that after a short time, it's easier to understand once again.

4 `2.13` **Listen to someone talking about the meaning of certain words in English. If there are things you don't understand, practise staying cool!**

LISTENING

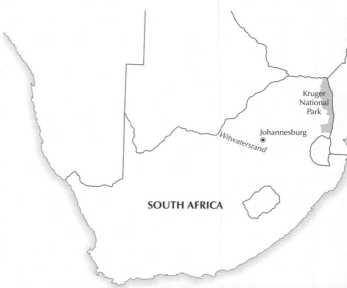

Kruger
National
Park

Johannesburg
Witwatersrand

SOUTH AFRICA

5a `2.14` Listen to this business presentation about South Africa. Which areas of the economy does the speaker talk about? Which are described in the most detail?

banking   chemicals   communication
energy   ~~food~~   mining   production of cars
ships   tourism   transport

food _____

5b Correct the mistakes in these sentences.

1 In the last 20 years, South Africa has developed into a modern industrial country.

  In the last 50 years, South Africa has developed

  into a modern industrial country.

2 South Africa's main trading partners are the USA, the UK, Japan, China, France and Germany.

  _____

  _____

3 South Africa's mining operations are concentrated in the north-west of the country.

_____

_____

4 Some mines go down to 2,000 metres.

_____

_____

5 South Africa has faced growing competition from Russia and America.

_____

_____

6 South Africa is now one of the most popular tourist destinations in the world.

_____

_____

7 South African cars and buses are exported to many Asian countries.

_____

_____

8 South Africa exports fruit, but not vegetables, all over the world.

_____

_____

GRAMMAR: present simple passive

6 Complete these sentences with a passive form of the verb.

1 Fish _is sold_ to Japan by Vietnamese companies. (sell)

2 Fifty percent of the world's clothes _____ in China. (make)

3 Fortunately, the city _____ by pollution. (not, affect)

4 When _____ from Zimbabwe to Europe? (flowers, fly)

5 Most of Pakistan's factories are near rivers, as water _____ for their processes. (need)

6 Where _____? (these products, send)

7 About half the USA's fruit and vegetables _____ in California. (produce)

8 More gold _____ for teeth in Japan than in any other country. (use)

TRANSLATION

7 Translate into your language. Notice the differences.

Gold is used in a wide variety of ways. The main use is in electronics – for example, in televisions and washing machines. The second most important use of gold is in teeth. Pure gold is not used because it is very soft. Instead, it is mixed with other metals. Gold is also found in pens and watches, and on perfume bottles and ceilings.

_____

_____

_____

_____

_____

_____

_____

_____

SPELLING: plural forms

8 Write the plural of these words.

1 tooth _teeth_   **6** woman _____
2 leaf _____   **7** volcano _____
3 photo _____   **8** cliff _____
4 factory_____   **9** potato _____
5 watch _____   **10** wife _____

9 Complete the words with _ie_ or _ei_.

1 I don't bel_ie_ve it!
2 Have you been to the new l__sure centre?
3 Gold leaf is used on c__lings.
4 She ach__ved a lot in her life.
5 He's my best fr__nd.
6 I must lost some w__ght!

SPELLING TIP

What can you do if you're not sure about the spelling of a word?

- When the sound of the vowel is the same as in 'believe' – write 'ie' (but write 'ei' after 'c', e.g. receive).
- In words where the vowel sound is not the same as in 'believe', the usual order is 'ei' (with the exception of 'friend').

VOCABULARY: business

1 Read the definitions and then complete the words.

1 to take something to a place
to d _e_ _l_ _i_ _v_ _e_ _r_

2 a business that sells things to the public
a r __ t __ __ __ __ r

3 to provide something
to s __ __ p __ __

4 to bring something into your country
to i __ __ __ r __

5 to send something to another country
to e __ __ __ r __

6 someone who purchases something
a b __ __ __ __ r

7 a famous make of a product
a b __ __ __ d

8 a business that makes things
a m __ __ __ f __ __ __ __ __ __ __ r

2 Complete the questions with the words in the box.

deliver	delivery	discount	much	offer
order	~~pay~~	price	time	

Cost

1 How much would you like to _pay_ ?

2 How _____ are they per item?

3 What's the _____ per item?

Delivery

4 What's the normal delivery _____ ?

5 We need _____ in two weeks. Can you do that?

6 When would you like us to _____ ?

Quantity and discounts

7 How many would you like to _____ ?

8 Can you _____ me a discount?

9 What _____ can you offer?

KEY LANGUAGE: negotiating

3 Read the negotiation between Richard and Lu Han and answer the questions.

1 What is Lu Han selling?

_____

2 How many does Richard order?

_____

3 What is the final delivery time?

_____

4a Complete the text with suitable words.

LU HAN: We're offering a great deal on digital cameras at the moment. It's the SLR300 model.

RICK: I see. How much are they per item?

LU HAN: Well, for you, how about $153 each?

RICK: $153? That [1] _seems_ rather high. I mean, it's not a famous brand, is it?

LU HAN: Really? I see. How much would you like to pay?

RICK: About $100.

LU HAN: Well, I'm not [2] _____ that we can go that low, but we can offer you discount. We can only offer a five percent discount on 1,000, but [3] _____ you order 2,000, we can offer 20 percent.

RICK: I see. That might be difficult. I'm not sure that we can sell 2,000. What about [4] _____ we order 1,500?

LU HAN: Well, then we can give you a 12 percent discount.

RICK: Hmm, that's still a [5] _____ low. How about 18 percent?

LU HAN: Eighteen percent? I'm [6] _____ we can't offer that.

RICK: Really? Well, okay then, I'll order 2,000 with the 20 percent discount.

LU HAN: Excellent news, a good decision. So, the final price is $122.40.

RICK: [7] _____ we call it $120? Keep it a round number, and we have ordered the music players already.

LU HAN: That [8] _____ fine. $120 per item it is, then.

RICK: Great, now, we need delivery in two weeks.

LU HAN: Two weeks? I'm afraid we [9] _____ do that. How about three weeks?

RICK: Okay, [10] _____ be fine.

LU HAN: Okay then. So, you order 2,000 SLR300 digital cameras [11] _____ $120 per item, and we deliver in three weeks. Is that a deal?

RICK: That's a [12] _____ .

4b `2.15` **Listen and check your answers.**

STUDY SKILLS: giving a short talk

1 These sentences are from two different presentations. Separate the presentations and write the extracts in the correct order.

1 Turning now to the shipping industry and key ports around the world, ...

2 To start with, I'd like to talk about the history of banking.

3 In conclusion, we can see that ships have a vital role in the global economy.

4 First, I'd like to talk about where ships are built.

5 To conclude, banking is an important part of any developed economy.

6 So, that was an overview of ship production.

8 Let's turn now to the services that a modern bank provides.

9 To sum up, banking has changed a lot over the years.

Presentation A ___4,_____

Presentation B _____

WRITING SKILLS: describing a process

2 Complete the sentences with the verbs in the present simple passive.

1 Coffee ___is made___ from beans which are found inside coffee berries. (make)

2 The berries _____ from the coffee bushes by hand. (pick)

3 The coffee beans _____ from the berry fruit. (separate)

4 The beans _____ (wash)

5 They _____ in the sun. (dry)

6 The beans _____ in large machines at a temperature of about 200°C. (roast)

7 The beans _____ in large 60kg bags. (put)

8 They _____ around the world. (ship)

3a Complete the description of coffee production with the sentences from Exercise 2.

Coffee: from the tree to the cup

¹ *Coffee is made from beans which are found inside coffee berries.* To begin with, ²_____ _____ and they are put in large water tank. Next, ³_____ and ⁴_____ _____ . Following this, ⁵_____ . After this, ⁶_____ . Next, ⁷_____ . Lastly, ⁸_____ _____ . This process varies in length according to the different tastes that are required. The longer the roast, the stronger the coffee.

3b Write a description of a simple process you know, e.g. How a cup of tea is made.

_____

_____

_____

_____

_____

_____

SPELLING: nouns ending -er or -or

4 Complete these nouns with -er or -or.

1 mana*ger*   6 competit____

2 administrat____   7 employ____

3 produc____   8 manufactur____

4 construct____   9 retail____

5 invent____   10 operat____

10.1 UNITED NATIONS

VOCABULARY AND SPELLING: people and organisations

1 Correct the spelling of the words in bold.

1 He's meeting the **ambasader** in the embassy.
  ambassador

2 Send the email to my **asisstent**. _____

3 When's the next meeting of the finance **comitee**? _____

4 I've got a new job in a different **dapartmant**. _____

5 The **spoksparson** is giving her presentation at 5.00 p.m. _____

6 The **Ministor** of Defence is abroad. _____

7 Who is the **Precidant** of the USA? _____

8 I'll tell the **stuff** the news about the changes in working hours soon. _____

GRAMMAR: present continuous for future arrangements

2 Complete the sentences with the verbs in the present continuous. Use contractions when possible.

1 What _are_ you _doing_ this weekend? (do)

2 I _____ my parents on Wednesday. (visit)

3 He _____ a rugby match on Saturday. (watch)

4 We _____ anything special tonight. (not do)

5 They _____ to the seaside on Sunday. (go)

6 She _____ tennis with Sarah on Tuesday. (not play)

EXTRA LANGUAGE

We can use the present continuous to talk about personal arrangements in/for the future.
I'm meeting Sarah at seven o'clock at the cinema.
We can use the present simple for the future when we talk about timetables. (not personal arrangements)
The film starts at 7.30.

3a Complete the dialogue with the present simple or the present continuous form of the verbs in the box.

arrive	~~do~~	finish	fly	go	have
leave	meet	start	take		

CAROL: What 1 _are_ you _doing_ this weekend?

TONY: Well, I 2_____ Silvio at the airport in the morning on Saturday. His plane 3_____ at seven o' clock, so I have to get up early to welcome him! Then, we 4_____ straight to the Guggenheim Art Gallery to see a special exhibition.

CAROL: Really? Don't you think Silvio will be tired after his flight?

TONY: Yes, I know it's a bit strange, but the exhibition 5_____ on Sunday and Silvio really wants to see it. After lunch, I 6_____ him to the Empire State Building.

CAROL: What about the evening? Have you arranged anything?

TONY: Well, we 7_____ dinner with Janice at 7.00.

CAROL: Okay, would you like to go to the cinema after that? *Gangs of New York* is on at the Rockefeller Center.

TONY: What time 8_____ the movie _____ ?

CAROL: At 9.00.

TONY: I think that's a bit late. We 9_____ to Washington in the morning. The plane 10_____ at 8.00. Why don't you have dinner with us tomorrow?

3b `2.16` Listen and check your answers.

READ BETTER: scanning for specific information

You don't always need to understand all the details in a text.

• Use key words or numbers to help you find the information.

READING

4 Read the headline and opening paragraph of a news article about International Aid. Then answer the questions.

1 What does OECD stand for?

_____

2 Which of these statements is false?

  a) Rich countries agreed to give a certain level of financial help to poor countries.

  b) The wealthy countries need to give more money to meet this target.

  c) The wealthy countries will never meet this target.

5 Quickly scan the rest of the article and answer the questions.

1 What should the level of aid be in 2010?

  $130bn (£66bn) a year

2 By how much is aid rising at the moment?

_____

3 By how much does it have to rise?

_____

4 What percentage of national income does the UN say rich countries should give?

_____

5 What percentage of national income does the USA give?

_____

6 Read the article again and answer these questions.

1 In which country is the headquarters of the OECD?

  France

2 When did the seven richest countries agree on the level of aid?

_____

3 How many countries have met the UN target?

_____

4 Which country gave the smallest percentage of its national income?

_____

5 Which country gave the largest amount of money?

_____

7 Find these words in the text. What do they refer to?

1 it (line 33) _____

2 their (line 36) _____

3 their (line 43) _____

4 its (line 55) _____

'West unlikely to meet aid targets,' says OECD
Larry Elliot, Economics Editor, February 22, 2007
Guardian Unlimited

RICH WESTERN COUNTRIES will only meet their promises of aid to the world's poorest countries
5 if they dramatically increase the level of financial assistance over the next three years, the Organisation for
10 Economic Cooperation and Development said today.

OECD, the Paris-based organisation, which has
15 30 members from the developed world, said that overseas aid will need to increase very fast in order to increase assistance to
20 $130bn (£66bn) a year by 2010, which is the amount that was promised before.

Despite the promises
25 made by the G7: the UK, the US, France, Germany, Canada, Italy and Japan, in July 2005, aid funding is not rising quickly
30 enough. Currently, it is rising at five percent a year, but the OECD says that it needs to rise by more than double that, 11
35 percent per year, in order to meet their promises.

Only a few countries, like Denmark, Norway, Sweden, Luxembourg
40 and the Netherlands met the United Nations target of donating at least 0.70 percent of their national income (GDP) to poor
45 nations. The average for the developed world was 0.33 percent.

Sweden and Norway both spent 0.94 percent of GDP in 2005, double
50 Britain's 0.47 percent contribution. The USA spent 0.22 percent of GDP on aid. However, the size of its economy meant that
55 it provided more money than any other country.

VOCABULARY: verbs from the text

1 Choose the correct verbs to complete the definitions.

1 to improve something; to make something bigger or better
to *develop/~~publish~~* new software

2 to plan something that you will build or create
to *support/design* a car

3 to make a new service available
to *launch/solve* an online shopping service

4 to make a new product available
to *release/respect* a film or a song

5 to produce a book for sale
to *design/publish* a novel

6 to say something is bad in some way
to *respect/criticise* someone's idea

7 to help or encourage someone or something
to *support/announce* a charity

8 to have a good opinion of someone
to *announce/respect* your President

9 to find the answer to something
to *solve/design* a complex problem

10 to say something in public
to *announce/launch* some good news

GRAMMAR: past simple passive

2 Complete these sentences with the past simple passive form of the verbs in brackets.

1 The children *were taken* to the zoo by their teachers. (take)

2 A bag _____ on the bus. (leave)

3 He _____ the computer by his parents. (not give)

4 I _____ how to drive by my brother. (teach)

5 We _____ the way to go by a policewoman. (show)

6 These televisions _____ in Japan. (not made)

7 How much _____ you _____ for your work yesterday? (pay)

8 _____ this picture _____ by Picasso? (paint)

9 All the money _____ on food. (spend)

10 The problem _____ by my assistant, not me. (solve)

EXTRA LANGUAGE

When we want to give the agent of an action in a passive sentence, we use 'by'.
This picture was painted **by** *Picasso.*

3 Change the active sentences into past or present simple passive sentences.

1 Many people respect Nelson Mandela.
   Nelson Mandela is respected by many people.

2 U2 released a new song last week.
   _____

3 The newspaper reviewers criticised the new film.
   _____

4 Apple develop new products every year.
   _____

5 They published *War and Peace* in 1869.
   _____

6 Bill Gates gave our charity $10 million last year.
   _____

LISTEN BETTER: taking notes

When you do a listening task, take notes.
- Concentrate on listening and try to follow the argument.
- After listening, use your notes to help you answer any questions.

4a Ask a friend to read you a short paragraph of no more than six lines. Write notes in your notebook.

4b Use your notes to rewrite the paragraph. Compare your paragraph with the original, and note the differences.

LISTENING

5a `2.17` Listen to the first half of a student talk about multinational corporations and take notes.

Hello, everyone. _____
_____
_____
_____
_____
_____

5b Use your notes to fill in the gaps. Use no more than three words and/or a number.

Introduction
Multinational corporations – **1** _positive_ or
2_____ effects
Part one
The number of multinationals has gone up over
the **3**_____
4_____ companies – Shell/Exxon
5_____ – Nike/Gap
technology companies – **6**_____
7_____ – Tesco/McDonald's
Branches in **8**_____ ,
make **9**_____
every year.

6a `2.18` Listen to the second half of the talk about multinational corporations and take notes.

_____
_____
_____
_____
_____

6b Use your notes to fill in the gaps. Use no more than three words and/or a number.

Part two
Local companies can't compete – they **1** _close down_
Local jobs **2**_____
Multinational's profits don't
3_____ that country.
Part three
People all over the world get
4_____ and services
5_____ may get better – pay
and **6**_____ for families/young
workers.
Conclusion
A multinational benefits a country if it looks
after its **7**_____ and
8_____ locally
9_____ is unavoidable.
We must ask for responsible
behaviour towards our
10_____ .

7 `2.17 & 2.18` Listen again to both parts of the talk and check your answers.

DICTATION

8 `2.19` Listen and complete the introduction in your notebook.

TRANSLATION

9 Translate into your language. Note the differences.

1 She is meeting the president at three o'clock tomorrow.

_____

2 He is travelling to France this Saturday.

_____

3 The minister isn't visiting our department on Friday.

_____

4 What are you doing this evening?

_____

2.20

VOCABULARY: words from the lesson

1 Choose the correct words to complete the sentences.

1 The athletes' ~~venue~~/accommodation will be single rooms in large flats.

2 The main stadium/accommodation will have 20,000 seats.

3 There will be a comprehensive/magical transport system, including buses and trains.

4 Half of the ten sports venues/stadiums need to be built.

5 We want to create a comprehensive/magical atmosphere.

6 We want to encourage/modern children to play sport.

7 We already have many world-class/comfortable sports facilities.

8 The rooms will be modern and comfortable/comprehensive.

KEY LANGUAGE: adding emphasis

2 Choose the correct position in each sentence for the words in brackets.

1 The hotel is _only_ five _____ minutes from the main stadium. (only)

2 At night, there is an _____ atmosphere _____ in the city centre. (electrifying)

3 It is _____ a _____ short drive to the countryside. (just)

4 The team's _____ performance was _____ amazing. (just)

5 The transport system includes a _____ train service _____ . (high-speed)

6 We _____ need to build two _____ new venues. (only)

7 _____ ten percent of the athletes will be in _____ double rooms. (just)

8 There are _____ two months until the Olympics _____ starts. (only)

PRONUNCIATION: pausing and emphatic stress

3 2.20 Listen to the presentation and mark the pauses (/) and underline the words with extra stress.

Ladies and gentleman, / thank you for coming to Spain's presentation to be the football World Cup hosts in 2022. Our presentation is based around three key points. First, Spain has a great football tradition. Because of this, we can offer world-class stadiums and fantastic training facilities. Secondly, we have millions of football fans in our country. The passion and support of these fans creates electrifying atmospheres at the matches. Finally, Spain has a comprehensive transport system. All the stadiums are only one hour from international airports and they are all served by public transport. Spain is the ideal choice for the World Cup in 2022.

PUNCTUATION

4 Correct the punctuation in these sentences, using capital letters, commas, and full stops. There are three sentences.

the united nations is an organisation that works in many different areas in order to carry out this work the un has a large department of international civil servants the secretariat the head of this un department is the secretary general and there are about 9000 other staff members

_____

_____

_____

_____

_____

_____

STUDY SKILLS:
improving your listening

1 Complete the advice with the words in the box.

| details | ~~general~~ | knowledge | list | predict |
| questions | topic | vocabulary |

1 Read the question carefully. Do you need to listen for the _general_ idea or for specific _____ ?

2 Before you listen, activate your _____ about the _____ . What do you know already?

3 Try to _____ what the speaker will say. Think of some _____ you think the speaker will answer.

4 Try to predict what _____ the speaker will use. Write a quick _____ of words before you listen.

2 Look at these importance markers. Put the words in the correct order.

1 out let that me point

   Let me point out that ...

2 that don't forget

   _____ ...

3 your I must attention this to draw

   _____ ...

4 is one of priorities our

   _____ ...

5 area another is important

   _____ ...

6 is another priority key

   _____ ...

7 the is thing important most we do

   _____ ...

WRITING SKILLS:
a for and against essay

3 Put the sentences in the correct order to make an essay. There are four paragraphs.

paragraph 1 (introduction) _F_ __

paragraph 2 (advantages) __ __ __ _A_

paragraph 3 (disadvantages) __ __ __ _H_

paragraph 4 (conclusion) __ __ __ _G_

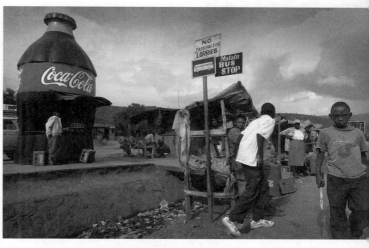

The advantages and disadvantages of global travel

A The transport industry provides employment for millions of people, and visitors spend a lot of money in the countries that they visit.

B Air travel causes a lot of pollution and hotels are often built in areas of natural beauty.

C One advantage is that people can visit countries that are very different to their own.

D This means that they can understand different cultures and be more tolerant of different people.

E Therefore, we need to think carefully before we travel around the world.

F Since the 1950s, global travel for both tourism and business has increased dramatically; every day there are millions of people travelling the world.

G Personally, I think the advantages are greater than the disadvantages, especially when we consider how important tourism is for many poorer countries.

H For example, restaurants begin to sell food that the visitors like, or the same shops are found in different countries.

I Another negative thing is that countries become more similar to each other.

J This is an important issue. This essay will consider whether global travel is good or bad for the world.

K To conclude, there are both advantages and disadvantages of global travel.

L Although we learn a lot by visiting different countries, we also change or damage the countries that we visit.

M Another positive thing about global travel is that it is good for the economy.

N On the other hand, a major disadvantage is that international travel can be bad for the environment.

11 The environment

11.1 GLOBAL WARMING

1 Complete the paragraph with the words in the box.

> atmosphere   ~~climate~~   fossil fuels   glaciers
> global warming   polar bears   rainforests
> sea ice   sea levels   temperature

Although the Earth's [1] *climate* has often changed for natural reasons, it has been changing more rapidly over the last hundred years. This rapid change is known as [2]_____ and it is caused by high levels of carbon dioxide in the [3]_____ due to the burning of [4]_____ . Because of global warming, many [5]_____ are melting and there is less [6]_____ in the Arctic. This means that [7]_____ are in danger of extinction and also that [8]_____ are rising, which means some Pacific Islands will soon disappear. The sea is also getting warmer, which is causing droughts in the [9]_____ . As well as this, coral reefs are dying because they are sensitive to [10]_____ changes.

**GRAMMAR:
present perfect continuous**

2 For each sentence write a second sentence with the same meaning. Use the present perfect continuous with *for* or *since* and the verbs in brackets.

1 The band started their concert an hour ago and they haven't finished.

   They've been playing for one hour. (play)

2 Sarah arrived at the bus stop 30 minutes ago. The bus has not come.

   _____ (wait)

3 Michael turned on the computer at ten o'clock. He is still using it.

   _____ (use)

4 You are on a round the world trip. You started it one month ago.

   _____ (travel)

5 It started snowing in the morning. It is still snowing now.

   _____ (snow)

6 Sam phoned Maria at eight o'clock. They are still on the phone now, at 9.30.

   _____ (talk)

3 Choose the correct verb to complete the sentences and questions.

1 I have *had / been having* my car for two years.

2 She has *been reading / has read* that book for two months.

3 We *have known / been knowing* each other for 15 years.

4 You have *been / been being* a teacher all your working life.

5 How long have we *been waiting / waited* for the bus? I'm bored now.

6 How long has he *been belonging / belonged* to that club?

TRANSLATION

4 Translate into your language in your notebook. Notice the differences.

Shona Harper is a biologist who has been working in the Brazilian rainforest for ten years. She has been studying the effects of global warming on the plants and animals that live in the rainforest. 'Recently, many trees have been dying because there has been less rain in the forest. I think there is less rain because the sea has been getting warmer. If this continues, there will be many fires in this area and we will lose much of the forest.'

READ BETTER: topic sentences

In many texts, the first sentence of a paragraph is the topic sentence – it tells you the main point or subject of the paragraph.

- If you need to read a text quickly to get a general idea of the contents, you can first just read the topic sentence of each paragraph. This will improve your reading speed, especially in exams.

5 Choose the best topic sentence for the paragraph in the READ BETTER box.

1 Paragraphs are important ways to organise a text. _____

2 You can improve your reading speed by concentrating on the opening sentences of paragraphs. _____

3 In different languages and cultures, paragraphs are written in different ways. _____

READING

6 Read only the topic sentences of each paragraph in this newspaper article. Then choose the best summary of the text a), b) or c).

7 Read the article again. Are these statements true or false or does the text not say?

1 The engineering ideas will be useful if we don't decrease our CO_2 production. _true_

2 In Norway, the CO_2 is removed when the natural gas is used. _____

3 The carbon removal methods could be very effective. _____

4 There are three ideas for reflecting more solar energy. _____

5 The space mirror is an expensive idea. _____

6 It is not difficult to control the cloud formation method. _____

7 Most of the ideas are dangerous for the planet. _____

8 Scientists mustn't create more problems with their solutions. _____

Can science save the day?

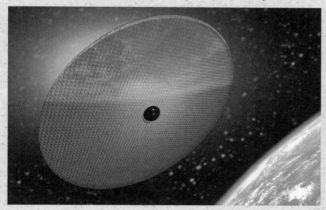

Scientists are thinking the unthinkable: can engineering projects save the world from global warming? How can we save the planet if we can't reduce our production of carbon? There are two main approaches to this question.

One approach involves the removal of carbon from fossil fuels. There are two ways to do this. The first involves removing carbon from the fuel before it is burnt. Currently, this happens in Norway where CO_2 is removed from natural gas as it comes out of the ground. The second involves capturing the CO_2 when it is produced by power stations. Both of these methods are expensive, but they could reduce the CO_2 produced by 90 percent.

The other approach is to reduce the amount of solar energy which hits the Earth. Some scientists have suggested putting a giant mirror in space. Others have suggested increasing the number of clouds over the oceans because they reflect back the sun's rays. This last technique has the advantage of being easy to stop and start.

There are many unanswered questions about these ideas, but they must be safe and not cause more damage. Any large engineering projects mustn't harm the Earth or the life on it. Otherwise, the cure for global warming might be worse than the original illness.

a) Scientists have had several ideas for fighting global warming, such as removing carbon from fuel. When the plans are finished, they will need to be safe and not expensive.

b) Scientists are designing engineering projects to fight global warming. There are two approaches: removing carbon from fossil fuels and reducing the solar energy that reaches the planet. The designs are not finished yet and should be safe.

c) If we can reduce the carbon in fuel or the solar energy that hits the Earth, we can win the fight against global warming. There are many possible solutions to the problem. Governments haven't decided which plan to follow, but they want plans that are safe.

WASTE NOT, WANT NOT

VOCABULARY: containers and materials

1 Choose the words which don't usually go with the containers.

1 a tube of *toothpaste/ointment/(water)*

2 a pot of *yoghurt/sugar/cream*

3 a can of *rice/beans/coke*

4 a bottle of *milk/meat/water*

5 a jar of *butter/mayonnaise/jam*

6 a packet of *rice/sugar/water*

7 a box of *chocolates/matches/milk*

8 a carton of *milk/fruit/fruit juice*

GRAMMAR: phrasal verbs

2 Choose the sentences a) or b) which have a phrasal verb.

1 a) I watched TV all weekend.

   b) Watch out! You're driving too fast.

2 a) I realised I was late when I looked at my watch.

   b) I looked after my neighbour's children because their mother was ill.

3 a) I carried out a lot of research for this article.

   b) I carried the baby out of the room as it was being noisy.

4 a) They went up the stairs when the police arrived.

   b) Last year, house prices went up a lot.

5 a) She held up the picture while he fixed it to the wall.

   b) She was late because the heavy snow held her up. She had to drive very slowly.

6 a) He picks up new languages easily – he only took a month to learn basic Chinese.

   b) He picked up the litter from the floor and put it in the bin.

3 Match the phrasal verbs in Exercise 2 with the definitions.

1 to do a task	*carry out*
2 to care for someone	_____
3 to increase	_____
4 to learn something informally	_____
5 to be careful	_____
6 to make something/someone late	_____

EXTRA LANGUAGE

Some phrasal verbs must have an object.

   1 *I carried out some research.*

   2 *He looked after the children.*

In sentence 1, you can put the object <u>between</u> the verb and the preposition or <u>after</u> the verb and preposition. This is a Type 1 phrasal verb.

   I carried some research out.
   I carried out some research.

If you use an object pronoun (*it, him, her* ...), you MUST put it between the verb and the preposition.

   I carried it out.   ~~I carried out it.~~

In sentence 2 you NEVER put the object between the verb and the preposition. This is a Type 2 phrasal verb.

   He looked after the children.
   ~~He looked the children after.~~

4 Find the incorrect sentences and correct them.

1 Type 1: Have you given back it to José?

   Have you given it back to José?

2 Type 1: I always keep my photographs. I never throw away them.

   _____

3 Type 2: The burglar broke the house into at night.

   _____

4 Type 2: It's a difficult problem. The committee will look into it.

   _____

5 Type 1: He's good at Spanish. He picked it up quickly.

   _____

6 Type 1: The bad weather held up her.

   _____

7 Type 1: When did you set your company up?

   _____

8 Type 2: What do you think her latest book of?

   _____

LISTEN BETTER: synonyms

Many listening tasks test your understanding of synonyms – words with similar meanings.

• Before you listen, look carefully at the questions and predict some synonyms for key words.

5 Replace the words in bold with synonyms from the box.

> a supermarket   customers   ~~is employed by~~
> litter   reuse carrier bags   solutions

1 The speaker **works for** _is employed by_ **a food shop** _____.

2 The speaker thinks **shoppers** _____ should **use their plastic bags several times** _____.

3 The speaker says there are two **answers** _____ to the problem of **rubbish** _____.

LISTENING

6 [2.21] **Listen to a radio discussion about recycling in New Zealand and choose the best description.**

Lindsay is on the radio ...

a) to encourage people to start recycling

b) to inform people about how to recycle

c) to explain what happens to recycled stuff

7 [2.21] **Listen again and choose the best answers a) or b).**

1 People should recycle because ...

~~a) they can save money and reduce pollution.~~

b) there is no space for all the rubbish.

2 The recycling scheme involves ...

a) people taking their recyclable waste to special recycling sites.

b) people putting rubbish in different kinds of container at home.

3 In the red bin, people should put waste that ...

a) is impossible to recycle.

b) is recyclable.

4 In the blue bin, people should put ...

a) small plastic bottles.

b) large plastic bottles.

5 Plastic bags ...

a) go in the blue bin.

b) should be used again and again.

6 People should put newspapers ...

a) in front of their homes.

b) in the red bin.

DICTATION

8 [2.22] **Listen and write the interview in your notebook.**

SPELLING: adjectives

9 **Some of these words are spelt incorrectly. Correct the words.**

1 availabel   _available_

2 horrible   _____

3 responsible   _____

4 suitible   _____

5 likeable   _____

6 incredable   _____

7 comfortabal   _____

8 flexeble   _____

9 believible   _____

10 reliable   _____

VOCABULARY: words from the lesson

1 Complete the table with eight nouns and seven adjectives.

annual	antisocial	community	crime
derelict	financial	graffiti	improvement
litter	run-down	scruffy	urban
volunteers	wasteland	youth club

Nouns	Adjectives
improvement	antisocial

2 Choose the correct word to complete the sentences.

1 This project will bring the local wasteland / community together.

2 We need more trees in urban/annual areas like city centres.

3 It's an expensive project, it will need a lot of run-down/financial support.

4 The children need places to go, like a youth club/ crime.

5 The canal is really scruffy/anti-social. We should tidy it up.

6 We should fine people who drop litter/graffiti on the streets.

7 Can we replace the annual/derelict buildings with new ones?

8 The project was set up by volunteers/improvement.

KEY LANGUAGE: question tags

3a Complete the statements with the correct question tag.

1 It's a lovely day, _isn't_ it?

2 You're from Spain, _____ you?

3 He'll help me, _____ he?

4 She won't come to the party, _____ she?

5 They haven't been here before, _____ they?

6 We could collect her, _____ we?

7 You think it's a good idea, _____ you?

8 It doesn't work, _____ it?

9 He's got a car, _____ he?

3b 2.23 Listen and check your answers.

EXTRA LANGUAGE

There are two possible intonation patterns for question tags.

- Use a falling intonation when you expect the listener to say yes.
- Use a rising intonation when you are asking a real question – when you want to check whether your idea is correct or not.

PRONUNCIATION: intonation in question tags

4 2.23 Listen again and repeat the sentences in Exercise 3a. Does the speaker use a rising or falling intonation? Write the answers.

1 _falling_

2 _____

3 _____

4 _____

5 _____

6 _____

7 _____

8 _____

9 _____

STUDY SKILLS: exploring reading texts

1 Read the text below and answer the questions.

1 Where did the text appear?
a) a national newspaper   b) a local newspaper

2 What type of text is it?
a) a news report   b) a letter   c) an advertisement?

3 Who wrote it and who will read it?

4 What is it about?

5 Why was it written?

2 Answer these questions in your notebook.

1 Which information is fact, which is opinion?

2 Which reasons does the writer give for building the phone masts?

3 Are there any reasons that the writer does not mention?

4 Which disadvantages of the phone masts does the writer mention?

5 Does the writer say exactly where they will build the masts?

6 Are there other possible problems that are not mentioned?

7 Why does the writer often use the words 'you' and 'we'?

8 Which phrases suggest Truefone is doing things for the local people?

Truefone: improving our service to you, the people of Glenloch

Ninety percent of Scotland has now got a good mobile phone service. However, ten percent of the country still has no mobile telephone service. Unfortunately, Glenloch is part of that ten percent.

At Truefone, we want to give you, the people of Glenloch, a modern mobile telephone service so that you too can use mobile phones and make video calls, and so that tourists can call local businesses.

In order to give you what you want, we need to build two mobile telephone transmitter masts in the town.

But don't worry, you will never see these telephone masts. Why? Because we will make them look like trees. The only thing you will notice is how good your phone service is.

We hope you will support our plans at the council meeting next week.

WRITING SKILLS: a report

3 Complete the report with the missing words and the correct form of the underlined verbs. Write your answers in your notebook.

Mobile phone masts in Glenloch: the people's view

Introduction

The aim ^{1} _of_ the report ^{2} <u>be</u> ∧ _is_ to summarise the findings ^{3}_____ a recent survey among the local residents of Glenloch on plans ^{4}_____ build two mobile telephone masts in the town. The data ^{5} <u>collect</u> by interviews with 1000 local residents ^{6}_____ 8 January and 15 January 2008.

Arguments for the mobile phone masts

A majority ^{7}_____ residents (62 percent) said that they ^{8} <u>support</u> the plan. The main reason (mentioned by 90 percent) was that they ^{9} <u>need</u> a mobile phone ^{10}_____ social and work reasons. Another important reason (given by 52 percent) ^{11}_____ that parents wanted their children ^{12}_____ have mobile phones for their personal safety.

Arguments against the mobile phone masts

A minority ^{13}_____ the residents (38 percent) ^{14} <u>feel</u> ^{15}_____ the plan was a bad idea. The main reason (given by 80 percent) ^{16}_____ that mobile phone masts could damage people's health. The other reason (mentioned by 60 percent) was ^{17}_____ masts could look ugly ^{18}_____ ruin the town's historic appearance.

Conclusion

To sum up, while ^{19}_____ was a lot of support for the plan for the two mobile phone masts, ^{20}_____ was also some opposition. This opposition ^{21} <u>concern</u> the exact locations ^{22}_____ the masts and possible effects on health. We recommend that a second survey ^{23} <u>carry out</u> once the possible locations ^{24} <u>know</u>, before a final decision ^{25} <u>make</u>.

12 Sport

12.1 MINORITY SPORTS

VOCABULARY: sports

1 Complete the sentences with the correct form of *do*, *go* and *play*.

1 I used to *play* hockey at school.

2 I've never _____ archery, but I'd like to try it.

3 He's going to _____ dragon boat racing next week.

4 We'd _____ table tennis if we had a table!

5 They _____ fencing every weekend.

6 Last year on holiday, I _____ sailing.

7 She's _____ badminton tonight.

8 You should _____ judo; it builds self-confidence.

9 He watches a lot of football, but I've never seen him _____ it!

10 Did you _____ gymnastics at school?

GRAMMAR: second conditional

2 Write complete sentences using the contracted form of *would*.

1 If I find / mobile phone / road, I / give / police

   If I found a mobile phone in the road, I'd give it to the police.

2 If I / not have / car, I / cycle / work

   _____

3 He / buy / football team / if he / have / lot / money

   _____

4 If you / come / class / every day, you / not find / the exams difficult

   _____

5 If we / not have / mobile phones, life / be / more difficult

   _____

6 If I / you , I / complain about your holiday

   _____

3 Put the words in the correct order to make questions. Then answer the questions in your notebook.

1 What you would buy if a millionaire were you ?

   What *would you buy if you were a millionaire?*

2 If in your was a fire house there, which take would two things you with you ?

   If _____ ?

3 If anywhere you live in the world could, you where choose would ?

   If _____ ?

4 What would have you problems if read you couldn't ?

   What _____ ?

5 What do you would if your a competition sports team favourite won ?

   What _____ ?

6 How would lost you if your feel job you ?

   How _____ ?

SKILLS IN ACTION

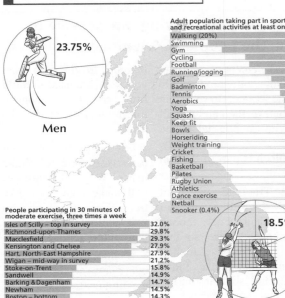

Men 23.75%

Women 18.5%

Adult population taking part in sport and recreational activities at least once a month	
Walking (20%)	8,142,693
Swimming	5,625,539
Gym	4,722,762
Cycling	3,175,650
Football	2,910,684
Running/jogging	1,872,819
Golf	1,457,347
Badminton	900,332
Tennis	874,040
Aerobics	608,671
Yoga	559,671
Squash	500,679
Keep fit	437,840
Bowls	407,135
Horseriding	401,916
Weight training	393,932
Cricket	380,366
Fishing	281,083
Basketball	275,028
Pilates	270,071
Rugby Union	267,817
Athletics	244,281
Dance exercise	204,737
Netball	163,504
Snooker (0.4%)	163,504

People participating in 30 minutes of moderate exercise, three times a week	
Isles of Scilly – top in survey	32.0%
Richmond-upon-Thames	29.8%
Macclesfield	29.3%
Kensington and Chelsea	27.9%
Hart, North-East Hampshire	27.9%
Wigan – mid-way in survey	21.2%
Stoke-on-Trent	15.8%
Sandwell	14.9%
Barking & Dagenham	14.7%
Newham	14.5%
Boston – bottom	14.3%

4 Look at these graphics and answer the questions.

1 Is the information only about sport?

No, it is about sport and recreational activities.

2 Does the information include children's habits?

_____

3 How often do the people do the activities in the survey?

_____

4 Put these activities in order of popularity?

pilates   netball   going to the gym   badminton

_____

5 Where do people do the most exercise?

Macclesfield   Sandwell   Isles of Scilly

_____

6 Who plays more sport, men or women?

_____

READING

5 Which of the questions in Exercise 4 does the newspaper article answer?

_____

6 Read the article again and answer the questions.

1 What percentage of the population don't play sport?

Fifty percent.

2 In general, which part of the country exercises the most?

_____

3 What social factor affects participation in sport?

_____

4 What does the government think people have to do?

_____

5 What does Sue Tiballs want newspapers to do?

_____

6 Do you think Sue Tiballs is optimistic about the future situation?

_____

SPELLING: nouns

7 2.24 Listen and write the words.

1 *population*   6 _____
2 _____   7 _____
3 _____   8 _____
4 _____   9 _____
5 _____   10 _____

Sports survey shock

THE ENGLISH MAY BE obsessed with sport but for half the population this only involves picking up the TV remote control. A study of nearly 364,000 people, commissioned by *Sport England*, reveals half of the adult population do no exercise at all. The survey reveals just one in five adults do sport or recreational activities for 30 minutes every week.

The top three activities are walking, swimming and going to the gym. Amongst the more minority sports, nearly a million people play badminton at least once a month, compared to netball which has just over 150,000 regular players. Pilates is a growing activity with nearly 300,000 participants.

The results also show a general difference between the north and the south of the country. It seems that more sport is played in the south than in the north. However, there are exceptions to this general rule. For example, the London Olympics will take place in one of the least sporting parts of the country;

only 14.5 percent of the population in East London do 30 minutes of exercise a week.

Sports participation is lowest in the poorest parts of the country. These results might make the government improve sport facilities in poor areas. The sports minister said the results were disappointing. 'We have invested £30bn in sports facilities over the last ten years. However, individuals must start to take responsibility for their health. We can't force people to switch off the TV,

get up from the sofa and do sport.'

More men take part in sport than women, 27.3 percent compared with 18.5 percent. Sue Tiballs, of the Women's Sports Foundation, said the results were shocking. 'Media coverage dedicated to women's sport is almost non-existent. Until these issues are addressed, and the perception that doing sport and exercise is a 'male' pursuit is altered, we are concerned that the number of women taking part will remain at these worrying levels.'

VOCABULARY: words from the lesson

1 Complete the phrases with the correct prepositions in the box.

at	about	~~on~~	of	in	for	on	on

1 to watch something _on_ a big screen

2 to aim an advertisement _____ someone

3 the majority _____ the TV audience was female

4 to be interested _____ people who dislike the game

5 to forget _____ female fans

6 to spend money _____ advertising

7 to focus _____ advertising to men

8 to make adverts _____ car tyres

GRAMMAR: *too* and *enough*

2 Which of these sentences are correct? Rewrite the incorrect ones.

1 You haven't got time enough. You're going to miss the train.

   You haven't got enough time. You're going to miss
   the train.

2 Have you got money enough for the holiday? New York is expensive.

   _____

3 It's too hot in here, I'm going turn the heating down.

   _____

4 He isn't enough busy. Give him more work to do.

   _____

5 There isn't enough space for that table in this room.

   _____

6 There is too sport on TV. I want to see more dramas.

   _____

EXTRA LANGUAGE

We often use verbs after phrases with *too* and *enough*.

*She is clever enough **to go** to university.*

*I am too tired **to play** football.*

3 Complete the sentences with the words in the box.

money	young	old	~~tired~~	clever
strong				

1 He's too _tired_ to walk any further.

2 They're too _____ to vote in the election.

3 He has enough _____ to buy an expensive car.

4 Grandad is too _____ to go on an adventure holiday.

5 Max is doing well at school. He's _____ enough to become a doctor.

6 She isn't _____ enough to lift her suitcase. Give her a hand.

4 Complete these sentences so that they are true for you.

1 I'm not rich enough to _____ .

2 I'm rich enough to _____ .

3 I'm strong enough to _____ .

4 I'm not old enough to _____ .

5 I'm too lazy to _____ .

LISTEN BETTER: understanding emotion and feelings

You can use the speaker's intonation and tone of voice to help you understand how they feel about something.

- When you listen, think about how the speaker is feeling. Is he/she happy or sad? Is he/she bored or excited?

5 `2.25` **Listen to the same sentence repeated three times. Choose the correct emotion from the box.**

| angry   disappointed   excited |

'I can't believe that you did that.'

1 _____

2 _____

3 _____

LISTENING

6 `2.26` **Listen to five sports fans talk about some recent sports events. Match the adjectives with the speakers.**

| bored   ~~disappointed~~   excited   worried
angry |

1 Speaker 1 feels *disappointed*

2 Speaker 2 feels _____

3 Speaker 3 feels _____

4 Speaker 4 feels _____

5 Speaker 5 feels _____

7 `2.26` **Listen again and complete the statements.**

1 Speakers *1* and ___ are talking *after* a sports event.

2 Speakers ___ and ___ are talking *before* a sports event.

3 Speaker ___ is talking *during* a sports event.

8 **Read the statements. Are they true, false or does the speaker not say?**

Speaker 1

1 His team scored some goals. *false*

2 His team put a lot of effort into the game. _____

3 In general, the other team is the better team. _____

Speaker 2

4 She has a good place to sit and watch the game. _____

5 Her team is weaker than the other team. _____

6 The captain of her team is the best player. _____

Speaker 3

7 Andy has played a game recently. _____

8 Andy has been a top player for some time. _____

9 Andy has been improving recently. _____

Speaker 4

10 It is unusual for this team to lose. _____

11 The team manager makes poor choices. _____

12 The team manager doesn't encourage the players well. _____

Speaker 5

13 The race is two hours long. _____

14 The Toyota team are currently in third place. _____

15 The speaker watches these events regularly. _____

DICTATION

9 `2.27` **Listen and complete the text.**

My local team _____

_____

_____

_____

_____

_____

_____ Come on you reds!

VOCABULARY: personality types

1 Complete the personality adjectives.

1 Football would suit a s _o_ c _i_ _a_ b _l_ e personality.

2 White-water rafting would suit a
r __ __ k - s __ __ k __ __ __ personality.

3 Yoga would suit a
n __ __ - c __ __ p __ __ __ t __ __ __ personality.

4 Rugby wouldn't suit an
i __ __ __ v __ d __ __ __ __ __ t __ c personality.

5 Athletics would suit a c __ __ p __ t __ __ __ v e personality.

6 Snowboarding wouldn't suit a c __ __ t __ __ __ s personality.

KEY LANGUAGE: conversation fillers

2 2.28 **Listen and complete the exam interview with the conversation fillers in the box.**

| let me see (x2)   let me think   right |
| that's a difficult question   to be honest   ~~well~~ |

I: So, are you interested in films and cinema?

s: ¹ _Well_ , I go to the cinema quite often. I like going with my friends to watch the latest films.

I: Such as?

s: Hmm, ² _____ … Hollywood films I suppose, you know, comedies and action films.

I: I see. Which do you prefer, going to the cinema or watching DVDs at home?

s: Well, ³ _____ . I have got a DVD player and I use it a lot, but which do I prefer? ⁴ _____ , erm, I think I prefer going to the cinema because it's a good way of seeing my friends.

I: Do you think the cinema is expensive?

s: Hmm, ⁵ _____ , I don't think it's too expensive. My local cinema is quite cheap and I don't go to the expensive cinemas in the city centre.

I: Would you change anything about your local cinema?

s: ⁶ _____ , well, I think I'd improve the food that's sold there. I think they should sell things like chips and hotdogs. What else? ⁷ _____ , no, I think that's all I'd change.

I: Okay, well thank you and that's the end of the interview. Send the next student in, please.

PRONUNCIATION: intonation in lists

3 2.29 **Listen and repeat these lists using the correct intonation.**

1 For this recipe I need to get some tomatoes, some olives, some chilli and some pasta.

2 There are three choices: a) buy a car, b) buy a house, or c) buy a boat.

3 Three students were absent today: Igor, Mohammed and Tina.

4 I'm very busy. I've got write an email, make two calls, book a hotel and book a flight.

5 We offer many activities including tennis, yoga, football and sailing.

TRANSLATION

4 **Translate into your language. Note the differences.**

'What would I do if someone gave me ten thousand dollars?' That's a good question! First of all, I'd say thank you very much. Then, I'd buy a ticket and I'd travel around the world for a year. If I could, I'd take my friend Ali with me. If he had the chance to travel, he would leave his job immediately. We'd visit every continent, including the Antarctic. It'd be amazing to go there.'

_____

_____

_____

_____

_____

_____

_____

STUDY SKILLS: doing exams

1 Match the sentence beginnings 1–6 with the sentence endings a–h.

1 When you are preparing for your exams,

2 Don't do too many practice exams

3 Make sure you're not tired on the day of the exam.

4 Follow the instructions on the exam paper,

5 If you can use a dictionary in the exam,

6 Don't spend too long on a question.

7 If you don't know the answer to a multiple-choice question,

8 When you are doing a writing question,

a) because after a while you don't learn anything new. ____

b) Don't stay up late the night before. ____

c) and make sure you understand the questions. ____

d) make a guess. ____

e) Move onto another one and come back later. ____

f) make a revision timetable. _1_

g) only use it to check key words. ____

h) make sure you make a plan before you write. ____

WRITING SKILLS: a formal email

2 The language in this email is too informal. Change the words and phrases in bold to make the email more formal. Rewrite the email in your notebook.

> Hi
>
> **I fancy doing** a course in 'English with Business Studies' this summer. **I'm interested** in studying in Canada and your college seems ideal. **I've got loads** of information from your website, but I **want to** ask a few questions.
>
> **Number one**, if I stayed for six weeks, how many teachers would I have? **Number two**, are there any exams at the end of the course? **I want you to tell me if I'll** get a certificate from the college when I leave.
>
> **About the** business studies, I'm particularly interested in the marketing option. **Tell me** what topics that course covers.
>
> As I mentioned before, I am very keen on coming to Canada and **I'd like** to live in a private apartment. **Send me** some details about the one-bedroom flats that are available.
>
> **It'll be good to hear** from you.
>
> **Bye**
>
> Wu Hei

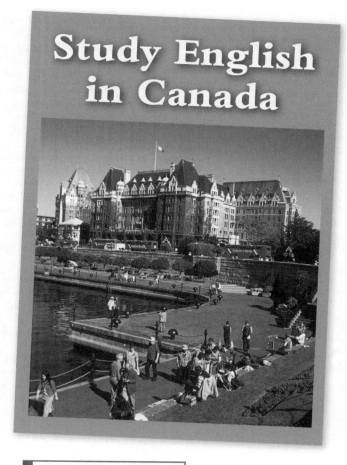

Study English in Canada

PUNCTUATION

3 Correct the punctuation in these sentences, using capital letters, commas, full stops, apostrophes and speech marks. There are three sentences.

for the last few weeks i have been travelling around the country talking to young people about minority sports the youngsters that i met were doing a wide variety of minority sports (e.g. fencing judo archery etc) and they were all enthusiastic and dedicated however they were also disappointed and angry about the lack of media interest in their sports and also about poor facilities and funding

_____

_____

_____

_____

_____

_____

_____

_____

_____

CD1
Lesson 1.2 Track 1.2
Anna, Brendon

A: You know, I'm going to Australia this summer. It's my first time.

B: Hey, that's great news, Anna. Of course, it's winter there then. [both laugh]

A: Yeah, I know that … er … actually, how long does winter last in Australia?

B: Well, generally speaking, from May or June to August. But it depends where you are.

A: What about in the south of the country? What's winter like there?

B: Well, in Victoria and Tasmania, the days are short and often chilly. And the nights are cold.

A: Does it snow?

B: Well, in most cities there's never any snow. It snows about once every ten years in Melbourne and Hobart, but it snows a lot in the mountains.

A: Where are they?

B: They're on the border between Victoria and New South Wales. We call them the Snowy Mountains – and it's not for nothing! Skiing's possible between June and October. Late August is a very popular time for skiing, but it's also very crowded. Actually … er … some people go to New Zealand instead – there's excellent snow and it's cheaper.

A: Is it true that some parts of Australia don't have any winter?

B: Yes, that's right. About 40 percent of Australia is tropical. You find that kind of climate in the north of the country, in Queensland and the Northern Territory. In June, July and August, the days are warm – great for swimming! And the nights aren't very cold. So, on the same day, in some parts of Australia people go swimming and in other parts they go skiing!

Lesson 2.2 Track 1.6
Presenter, Orla

P: Good evening and welcome to the first Krzysztof Kiewlowski Film Festival here in the North-East of England. Over the weekend, you can see a very large number of films by this great Polish director and tonight the film critic Orla Murphy is here to introduce Kiewlowski's life and work. Welcome, Orla.

O: Thanks, Pat.

P: OK, Orla. Now, Kiewlowksi was born in Warsaw in 1941.

O: Right.

P: But his early life wasn't easy, I understand.

O: No, not at all. His father had a serious disease – tuberculosis actually and to find good treatment, the family moved from one small town in Poland to another. Kiewlowski himself wasn't a very healthy child.

P: I believe he read a lot.

O: That's right, yeah. He read a lot of books, everything from American cowboy stories to the great Russian novels by Dostoevsky. At an early age, he understood that life wasn't just the things you can touch or buy in shops. There was more than that.

P: So … how did he become a film-maker?

O: Well, in 1964, he entered the Lodz Film School. He made his first short films while he was studying there. After film school, he made a number of documentaries about the lives of ordinary people.

P: When did he make his first really important films?

O: In the late 1980s. Two of the films from this period are now very famous: *A Short Film about Love*, and *A Short Film about Killing*. They're about the lives of people in one building.

P: Was he still working in Poland at that time?

O: Yes, he was. He started to make films outside Poland in 1990.

Lesson 2.2 Track 1.7
Presenter, Orla

O: The first of those films was *The Double Life of Veronique*. It's about two women, one in Poland, and one in France, and the connection between their lives. Later, he made three films called: *Blue, White* and *Red*, the colours of the French flag, These films are about being free, being equal, and being kind to people.

P: Can we call him a European film-maker?

O: We can, but he was also Polish. And he was very proud of that.

P: Orla, Kiewlowski's later films were very successful. Lots of people went to see them. Why exactly?

O: Well, when people watched a film by Kiewlowski, they felt they were watching their own lives. Kiewlowski was asking the same questions as them: why get up in the morning? What's the meaning of life?

P: Thanks, Orla.

Lesson 3.2 Track 1.12
Speaker 1

Well, I think it's very important for them to do that. They need to learn about the world and major events – I'm sure it helps them with their schoolwork. However, you need to be careful sometimes because perhaps a story is not suitable for kids, you know, murder stories and things like that.

Speaker 2

Oh, both. When I wake up I watch the breakfast news shows – I like to know what is happening right now and they also tell you about major travel problems. Then, I buy a paper for my journey to work. I travel by train so I can read the stories carefully and get more details than I can from the television programmes.

Speaker 3

Well, I often watch them and I think they're quite good usually. In Britain, they're about thirty minutes long so they can give you a lot of good information. Sometimes I think there are a lot of stories about celebrities and films stars – I don't like those kinds of story, you know, about their relationships and lives. But, there is also a lot on international news, which I think is very important.

Speaker 4

Personally, I get a lot of my news online now. I check the BBC website four or five times a day while I'm at work. It's good because the news is up-to-date, you get the latest news and I prefer that. You know, the morning paper can only tell you yesterday's news, and that's old news really. I know there is more detail in the papers, but, I don't have time to read long articles.

Lesson 4.2 Track 1.16
Careers adviser, Nicki

CA: So, how can I help you?

N: Well, I'm interested in a career in health and food. I've seen three different job titles: a nutritionist, a dietician and a food scientist, but I can't see how they are different.

CA: Okay, well, first of all, after studying at university, a food scientist generally works in the food production industry. Generally, this job is not really about people's health, although that is important.

N: I see. Well, I'm more interested in health and diet.